I SIT ALL AMAZED

The Extraordinary Power of a Mother's Love

STEVE MIKITA

With a Foreword by Carole Mikita

DESERET
BOOK

SALT LAKE CITY, UTAH

All photographs courtesy of the Mikita family archives. Used by permission.

Library of Congress Cataloging-in-Publication Data
Mikita, J. Stephen, 1955– author.
    I sit all amazed : the extraordinary power of a mother's love / Steve Mikita ; foreword by Carole Mikita.
        pages cm
    Includes bibliographical references.
    ISBN 978-1-60641-938-0 (paperbound)
    1. Mikita, J. Stephen, 1955–   2. Mormons—Utah—Biography.   3. Spinal muscular atrophy—Patients—United States—Biography.   4. Children with disabilities—Care—Moral and ethical aspects.   5. Children with disabilities—Development—Case studies.   6. Christian biography—Mormon authors.   I. Title.
    BX8695.M54A3 2011
    289.3'32092—dc22
    [B]   2010045047

Printed in the United States of America
Malloy Lithographing Incorporated, Ann Arbor, MI

10 9 8 7 6 5 4 3 2 1

CONTENTS

Foreword v

Introduction 1

CHAPTER ONE
"My Son, Peace Be unto Thy Soul" 3

CHAPTER TWO
"In the World Ye Shall Have Tribulation" 20

CHAPTER THREE
"We Do Not Doubt Our Mothers Knew It" 32

CHAPTER FOUR
"Bow Down Thine Ear, O Lord" 48

CHAPTER FIVE
"The Tender Mercies of the Lord" 58

CONTENTS

CHAPTER SIX

"If Any of You Lack Wisdom, Let Him Ask of God"....... 69

CHAPTER SEVEN

"I Am Jesus Christ, Whom the Prophets
Testified Shall Come into the World" 87

CHAPTER EIGHT

"He Will Take upon Him the Pains
and the Sicknesses of His People" 103

CHAPTER NINE

"Peace I Leave with You, My Peace I Give unto You" 112

CHAPTER TEN

"That Your Joy Might Be Full" 123

Postscript 133

Sources Cited 135

FOREWORD

I have two memories that remain as clear to me as if they had happened today.

In 1955, I was only four, and I remember tiptoeing into my parents' bedroom to see my new baby brother, John Stephen. Mother let me sit in the big rocking chair and then she placed him in my arms. He was so warm; he felt just right. He had barely visible, wispy, blond hairs and big, blue eyes. He looked at me. What a feeling! I was thrilled. And then I made the connection between the kicking infant in Mother's tummy and the baby resting in my arms. I announced to Mother, "He is my baby." And ever since then, Steve has been a focal point for my love, admiration, and inspiration.

In the spring of 1961, I was nearly ten years old and the oldest of four children—me, Billy, Steve, and Judy. Mother and Dad had driven to Pittsburgh, forty miles from our home in Steubenville, Ohio, for dinner, a show, and an overnight stay in a downtown hotel. Our father's assistant drove us to meet them the next day, and

With Carole, mid-1990s.

when we got out of the car, there were our dynamic, loving parents, overjoyed to see their children.

Mother was breathtaking. I remember exactly what she was wearing, including her designer navy coat with a matching velvet hat—she was a Jackie Kennedy look-alike—and her radiant smile. She was more than a fashion statement, however. Mother was an intelligent, independent, and elegant woman, who was fervently committed to family, community, and God. I felt treasured by her. When I saw her that day, she glowed with assurance in her newfound faith as a Latter-day Saint. To me, this woman not only stole the show, she defined motherhood.

Steve and I are simply each other's best friends. We take care of each other, and I find great solace in his words and powerful testimony. He has endured much and has learned from that which he has been asked to experience during his time on Earth. He is a powerful and humble man who serves and lightens the burdens of others. I often come to him on days that are difficult, and we counsel together. Quite often we reflect on the lessons and principles we learned from our precious mother, and we come away refreshed and renewed. I have traveled the world on my assignments as a journalist, and I am always so anxious when I have to leave him and eager to hear his exultant voice upon my return.

I have met and interviewed fascinating people in my more than thirty years as a journalist—some famous, most not. Many have left positive impressions on my life, but none quite like my brother Steve. As a former boss of his once said, "It takes more energy for him to get out of bed in the morning than it does for the rest of us to work all day." He possesses many gifts, but his insight into life's challenges, his ability to not only envision solutions but to see the big picture through his wisdom and faith have given me countless hours of comfort and hope.

How our mother found the courage to become a Latter-day Saint against every family member's wishes, and how my brother rises above incredible physical disabilities to reach goals most people never dream of are stories you are about to discover.

Press on, dear reader, and meet two incredible, unforgettable people whom I love deeply.

—CAROLE MIKITA

INTRODUCTION

I was born with a relentless muscle disease. I have never walked, never run, never ridden a bicycle. I have never driven a car. I have never played a single round of golf, never close-danced, and never knelt to pray. I have never married. I have no children. But the story of my life and the lessons I've learned are not about those things that I have never done or will never do. That is not my purpose in writing this book. My life is not about getting weaker or waiting to die.

This story is about reaching our possibilities in spite of our disabilities. It is about realizing our dreams and achieving our goals, no matter what the obstacle, no matter what stands in our way. It is about choosing to thrive, not just survive.

It is not only about me. It is a book about the undeniable influence and power of a mother's love. It is a story about the difference that mothers make.

This book is about understanding how to live rich, meaningful lives—even though our lives can have very difficult and tragic turns. All of us experience things that we never predicted could or should happen to us. We all face challenges that weigh us down and try both our patience and our faith.

It is my hope that this book will help you face, bear, and even overcome the trials and tribulations in your life and your children's lives.

I have lived on this earth for fifty-three years. I grow weaker every year. But because of the strength of my faith and my testimony of Him who never tires and who never grows old, I become stronger and even more determined to share His message of hope and support.

By studying and, more important, by accepting His power and love, you may confront and overcome your challenges and crises. I know that to be true; and I want you to know that too.

How do I know these things? How did I come to know Him? How did I learn of His power to heal and to comfort? How do I know that He knows me? How do I know that He cares? How can I have faith, when my body continues to deteriorate and my muscles continue to atrophy?

How do I know after all these years of living my life in my wheelchair that He remembers me and has not forgotten me? Does He really understand me, when I feel alone or frightened? Is He still actually—and actively—involved in my life?

Does He know us by our names, or is He only a disinterested observer? Is He merely acquainted with our grievances and our sorrows, or does He *know*? How much does He know? How much does He care?

This book is not only about my experiences and my questions, but it is also about the answers to these questions that I received from my mother.

CHAPTER ONE

"MY SON, PEACE BE UNTO THY SOUL"

J ust as with every story, this story has a beginning. In the beginning, during her pregnancy with me, my mother, Mildred, experienced no warning signs or any clue that anything was different or wrong. Everything went smoothly. There was no hint that abnormality was on the horizon.

Prior to my birth, Mother and Dad's life appeared to be normal and happy. He was a driven and successful physician and father, and she was an active and loving mother of two healthy children, Carole and William. In fact, when the delivering physician pronounced me perfect, it simply confirmed to them that their good fortunes would continue and that they were being richly blessed. So far, so good. No need to worry. No cause for concern. Just another normal birth in the bustling steel town of Steubenville, Ohio. It was vintage 1950s Americana.

For the first several months of my life, I satisfied the predictable formula of babyhood. I was chubby, jolly, and irresistibly cute. I was

Mildred with her first three children:
Bill, me, and Carole, 1956.

lovable and I was loved. On schedule, I crawled, just like my peers. Crawling was a milestone previously reached by my siblings, and so it was accompanied by little or no fanfare. All babies crawl. Healthy babies crawl. But then suddenly the alarm of tragedy was triggered.

One day when I was six months old, I was playing on the floor when my father reached under my arms to lift me up. Unlike normally developing infants, my arms did not offer him a firm, resistant grip. Rather, they floated horrifyingly upward. As I slipped through his hands and fell to the floor, the bottom fell out of our happy home. Terror had trespassed upon my family's routine tranquility.

As a physician, my father instinctively knew that something was wrong. He had diagnosed other childhood diseases and immediately began to fear that I had some type of degenerative muscle disease.

He did not know exactly what disease, but he knew enough to know that his world and my life would never be the same.

Rather than disclose his findings and suspicions to my mother, he did what we all do when tragedy abruptly knocks at the door of our lives: Dad chose to hope against hope that he was wrong.

He tried to ignore the irrefutable evidence that I was not getting stronger. It soon became clear to both Mom and Dad that I was not progressing and achieving the milestones that babies my age should be reaching.

I was still crawling, but I was not weight-bearing. Every time I was coaxed to walk, all my parents witnessed was a baby yearning to walk, but not learning to walk.

I collapsed time and time again under my own weight. It must have been agonizing for Mother and Dad to watch me struggle. I never took one voluntary step. Not one.

Notwithstanding Mother's cheers and prayers, I demonstrated no inclination to stand under my own power, independent of a helping hand. It was impossible for me. The moisture on my head did not come from my trying to walk; it came from my mother's seemingly endless tears. To verify their findings and confirm their suspicions, my parents took me to the Children's Hospital in Pittsburgh.

I was examined by a neurologist, and then my father heard this diagnosis: "Dr. Mikita, your son does not need a neurologist; your wife needs a psychiatrist. If she simply backs off and quits pressuring Stevie to walk, he will walk any day."

Though I was fifteen months old and had never taken a single, solitary step under my own power, according to this doctor, my mother was being irrationally frantic about my lack of development; *she*—not I—was the problem.

Mother and Dad were so desperate to heed his inaccurate and reckless diagnosis that they gladly followed his advice. For the next three months, they simply waited for me to walk. Each day would dawn with renewed hope that their concern would end. But each day all they saw was their son content to sit on the floor.

When they tried to entice me to get off the floor, my uncooperative body rejected their efforts. According to what I have been told, I just sat, oblivious to the terror that had invaded their lives and the disease that had infected my muscles.

It was becoming transparent and painfully obvious: my inability to stand or walk was not an issue of *would* not, but rather *could* not. There was no lack of desire, only a lack of strength. Mother's mental health and anxiety had absolutely nothing to do with my growing incapacity.

But there were more questions than answers, and Mother and Dad needed some verification that I truly was different. They needed information. How long would I have this disorder? Would I ever walk? Was death looming over me? Would I ever reach adulthood? Would I live independently? Would I marry and father children? There were so many questions and no one had the ability to give my parents any peace of mind or concrete explanation for why this was happening or what the future would hold.

Days of hoping turned into weeks of frustration. My condition was not improving. I was not developing, and I was not showing any signs that I was simply a slow walker. Finally, three months after the initial diagnosis, Mother and Dad could not wait any longer. They were no longer willing to live with the uncertainty that shrouded their future and mine. They needed answers. Without knowing why I could not walk there was no way they could go on. It was time to seek a second opinion.

But at eighteen months, I remained a medical anomaly. There were no easy answers or explanations, and every physician they consulted was baffled by my advancing disability. There was no textbook

*I was approximately eighteen months old when I
was diagnosed with Werdnig-Hoffman's Disease.*

definition about why I simply could not sustain my own weight,
independent of someone holding my hands. Finally, my father contacted the National Institutes of Health in Bethesda, Maryland. He
had confidence that surely this revered and highly respected center
of medical research would be able to unlock the mystery of my unresponsive body. The appointment was made, and we boarded the
train in Ohio and set off for a trip that held more peril than promise.

For three days, I was subjected to a battery of strength and sen-
sitivity tests. I failed the strength tests—all of them. However, I was
not paralyzed; I could feel the needles the doctors inserted into my
legs and feet.

I, of course, have no memory of that time, but from what my
parents have told me, it must have been quite an ordeal. My parents
had to step out of the room as men in white coats surrounded me

and subjected me to the tests. I must have wished that my parents could have told these men to stop hurting me. Instead, they were scurried out of the room each time a new platoon of men walked in with their stoic facial expressions and the cold, primitive-looking tools that were used to probe and prick my body.

And then, at the end of those three days, there was a verdict. It was as unanimous and certain as it was devastating. This intimidating jury in white declared unequivocally that I had a neuromuscular disease; it even had a name: Werdnig-Hoffman's Disease. It was difficult to pronounce and even more difficult to comprehend. Furthermore, it was both incurable and fatal. It would almost certainly kill me before my second birthday! And there it was in all its awful horror—the truth.

I had no strength.

I had no future.

I had no cure.

I had no hope.

I had no treatment.

I was dying.

My parents were informed that I had only weeks left to live. Perhaps, if I were fortunate, a couple of months. That is not an optimistic prognosis for anyone, especially for an eighteen-month-old little boy who they only wished to take home where he could play with his brother, Billy. I didn't know why my parents were so sad. I just knew that they were.

We had traveled far from home with the glimmer of hope that I had been misdiagnosed or that somehow my body's downward spiral could be reversed. But instead, all hope was dashed and replaced with terror, devastation, and grief.

My parents had sought for a medical refuge and were met instead with a medical abyss. Death loomed over me and over them.

They had been delivered the horrifying news that their son was dying and no one or nothing would be able to prevent it. They had exhausted all avenues of rescue and hope. They had only two assignments left to fulfill: they needed to prepare for the birth of their fourth child, and, at the same time, they needed to prepare for the death and funeral of their third.

But then, miraculously, the darkness that permeated their lives and mine began to disappear. Light penetrated our home, and somehow, some way, hope was restored.

Mother and Dad observed that my condition was not deteriorating at the rapid pace predicted by the physicians back in Maryland. I was not getting any stronger, but neither was I getting any weaker. Inexplicably, I seemed to have reached a state of equilibrium. It was as if I had obtained some sort of physical reprieve—a stay of execution. I was neither sad nor in pain.

I was happy.

I was healthy.

I was alive.

Months went by. The anticipated downward spiral toward death was not occurring. Had there been a miracle? Would my life be spared, or had I simply been given a temporary reprieve? The short answer is that a miracle had happened. Not a cure. I was still not standing, walking, or running. I was not suddenly given a strong, active body. And, yet, because the disease was not progressing, hope remained. There appeared to be a future. There was both light and life despite my feeble physical condition.

By the time I reached my fourth birthday, I had already surpassed those doctors' prognoses by two full years!

I was not walking, but neither was I dying. I was destined to remain in that disabled condition, however, and the question became how I was to live with such a disability without the expected

The Mikita children: Carole, Billy, me
(four years old), and Judy.

attendant discouragement, unhappiness, and futility of such an existence. What was to become of me, and how would my family cope
with the responsibility to care and provide for me?

My answer came from a magazine! Not from a medical jour-
nal or a physician's reference guide to childhood diseases. It was just
an ordinary magazine that my father purchased from a newsstand,
but that April 1960 issue of *Look* magazine contained for me and
my family an extraordinary source of hope, power, and tenacity. It
featured photograph after photograph of President Franklin Delano
Roosevelt. It was a picture-by-picture celebration of what FDR had
accomplished in his life in spite of his disability. He was paralyzed
from the chest down, and yet he had not allowed his physical limitations to defeat him and destroy his life. He had, in fact, become the
president of the United States *after* he was diagnosed with polio.

Every morning for two years, I took my morning dose of

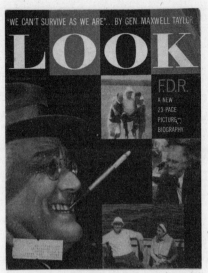

This issue of Look *magazine brought me hope and inspiration during a difficult time in my life.*

inspiration and motivation from my miracle magazine. I found more than hope by looking at those photographs of the disabled president. I had found my hero and my reason to live. I had found my future.

I did not feel so vulnerable and alone. There was someone I could look up to and to whom I could relate. I might be different from other people, but so was FDR. He had been a pioneer, of sorts. He had done things and achieved things that no other man with such a severe disability had ever accomplished. I was just a boy, and I was not the president, but I still had a life to live.

One day, my father closed the magazine we had been looking at. We were sitting on my bed. He lifted me onto his lap and raised my chin with his thumb and forefinger so that my eyes would meet his.

Dad said, "Stevie, you will never be able to walk and run like the other children because you have extremely weak muscles. But you have a strong mind.

"You will never play football, basketball, or baseball with other boys. But you can compete in the classroom and excel.

"You must never, ever feel sorry for yourself. You have been given a lot. You are better off than your two immigrant grandfathers—your namesakes—John and Stephen, who came to America when they were teenagers. After they left the Old World, they never saw their parents again. They had no money. They could not speak English. They were uneducated."

And then Dad concluded with this advice: "Don't be afraid, son. If FDR did it, then so can you."

That was the answer. That was the truth. Discovering the example of Franklin Delano Roosevelt was one of the critical turning points of my life. That was the future that my parents and I had been seeking.

Though both of us were unaware of it at the time, my father was echoing what the Prophet Joseph Smith learned during his ordeal in Liberty Jail.

On December 1, 1838, Joseph, along with his brother Hyrum, and four others—Lyman Wight, Caleb Baldwin, Sidney Rigdon, and Alexander McRae—were transported from Richmond, Missouri, where they had been incarcerated in a log cabin, to the dark and frigid chamber located in Liberty, Missouri. They remained there under spurious charges for nearly five unrelenting months of cruel and egregious treatment. To say that this was an awful and terrible trial understates the deprivation and extremity that they were forced to endure day and night.

For more than four months in the dead of winter, six men lived in a single room that measured no more than fourteen feet by fourteen feet. This dungeon featured only two small iron windows and a trapdoor to the upper floor. The men slept on a straw-strewn, dirt floor. Their food was purposely "filthy" and was characterized by

Joseph as "scant, uniform, and coarse" (Smith, *Personal Writings of Joseph Smith,* 417).

Besides these appalling conditions, the prisoners were under constant harassment by jeering onlookers who peered through the windows and treated them as if they were nothing more than circus animals. What was even worse was the torrent of obscenity and blasphemy that was not only directed toward them and their beliefs but also toward their wives.

By March 1839, even Joseph, in a letter to his beloved Emma, recognized that "my nerve trembles from long confinement" (Smith, *Personal Writings of Joseph Smith,* 409). It is no wonder that Joseph labeled Liberty Jail as a version of "hell" in which they were surrounded by "demons" (Smith, *History of the Church,* 3:290).

It was here amidst this terror that Joseph reached out through the darkness. His nerves must have been frayed and his emotions raw when he at last cried out:

> O God, where art thou? And where is the pavilion that covereth thy hiding place?
>
> How long shall thy hand be stayed, and thine eye, yea thy pure eye, behold from the eternal heavens the wrongs of thy people and of thy servants, and thine ear be penetrated with their cries?
>
> Yea, O Lord, how long shall they suffer these wrongs and unlawful oppressions, before thine heart shall be softened toward them, and thy bowels be moved with compassion toward them?
>
> O Lord God Almighty, maker of heaven, earth, and seas, and of all things that in them are, and who controllest and subjectest the devil, and the dark and benighted dominion of Sheol—stretch forth thy hand; let thine eye pierce; let

thy pavilion be taken up; let thy hiding place no longer be covered; let thine ear be inclined; let thine heart be softened, and thy bowels moved with compassion toward us.

Let thine anger be kindled against our enemies; and, in the fury of thine heart, with thy sword avenge us of our wrongs.

Remember thy suffering saints, O our God; and thy servants will rejoice in thy name forever. (D&C 121:1–6)

Joseph, who, as a boy of fourteen, had communed with the Father and the Son in a sacred grove of trees, was now crying out in his extremity for reassurance and comfort. He who had conversed with Gods, ancient prophets, and instructing angels, was grasping for any sense and purpose in the madness and oppression that he and his friends were being asked to endure.

Joseph's prayer was answered. And that answer was as simple as it was profound:

My son, peace be unto thy soul; thine adversity and thine afflictions shall be but a small moment;

And then, if thou endure it well, God shall exalt thee on high; thou shalt triumph over all thy foes. (D&C 121:7–8)

There came into that rank, squalid, cold, and dark dungeon a penetrating, reassuring light of everlasting hope to Joseph and to all of us: our mortal uncertainty and suffering are not to be of endless duration. Furthermore, by patiently enduring the trials that beset us, we acquire the attributes that will ultimately permit us to enjoy eternal life.

It is impressive to me that the Lord addressed Joseph as "my son." He who had created the heavens and the earth was aware of a man praying from a jail in an obscure Missouri town. A relationship—a kinship—was pronounced and proclaimed. Not only to Joseph, but to all of us. There is no distance. There is no detachment. There is interest. There is familiarity. There is family.

The Lord was present. He was near. He had not forgotten Joseph in jail. Then comes the phrase, "peace be unto thy soul." The Lord reaches into that cell and consoles Joseph in the depths of his depression.

It is significant to note that the Lord did not break down the walls of the jail. He did not paralyze the jailors or the mobs who were taunting and stalking Joseph and his followers. There was not a sudden change of heart among the persecutors. Joseph and his brethren were still surrounded by wicked and evil men. Joseph remained in jail. Prayer did not parole him.

He could have been freed; the Lord had the power. He is the Lord Almighty. He is omnipotent. But Joseph's trial, like our trials, was personal. This was about Joseph. This was about his calling, his mission, and his discipleship. This trial further defined a prophet's calling and refined a prophet's character.

But this prayer by the Prophet is about so much more than just Joseph and his calling. If Joseph had immediately and miraculously been saved or somehow rescued from the jail, you and I would have been deprived of one of the most precious scriptures in all of holy writ. Without this scene, our trials and our tribulations would be robbed of the perspective, the comfort, the love, and the nearness that only the Savior can and does bring us.

This was not something I fully understood as a child growing up with a debilitating disease. It is an understanding that I acquired later in life, after I had been introduced to The Church of Jesus Christ of Latter-day Saints and had come to know the history of the Restoration. The lesson I learned is that no matter where we are, who we are, or what set of circumstances combine to imprison us with feelings of great uncertainty, pain, and suffering, the Lord is ever mindful of us and will ultimately deliver us from our infirmities.

If those jail walls had been torn down by a legion of angels, then you and I might immediately think, "Joseph was saved because Joseph was the anointed. He was chosen before this world was to usher in the Restoration of the Lord's true and living gospel. He was and is the Prophet. The Lord knew Joseph and watched over him ever since he entered the Sacred Grove. Of course the Lord would not abandon His servant."

If Joseph had been miraculously delivered, we might also have reasonably concluded, "Miracles do not happen to me. I am too undeserving. I am too disobedient. I am too far away for the Lord to notice or to care about me. My problems are too insignificant. I am too unimportant. My problems do not compare to the Prophet Joseph Smith's."

We would dismiss the entire narrative as being foreign to us. We simply could not relate to a prophet who had seen so much and learned so much throughout his tenure on earth. We would find little or no solace from his story.

But the fact of the matter is that Joseph wasn't immediately saved. He was allowed to stay in jail. But he was taught by the things he endured, just as we are taught by what we endure. He was comforted; we can be comforted. He was reminded of who he was; we are reminded of who we are. He was reassured of who was on his side; we are reassured of who is on our side. He learned who was listening to him; we learn who is listening to us. Explaining to Joseph how the ordeal would be useful, the Lord said, "Thine adversity and thine afflictions shall be but a small moment" (D&C 121:7). The Lord recognized and realized that Joseph was suffering. But this was his adversity and his affliction. That means that each of us, as Joseph did, have trials and pains that are unique to our earthly missions. They are ours. They are individually tailored to teach us, remind us, and return us to Him. Most of the time we do not escape them. That is not how it works.

What does "a small moment" mean? Sixty seconds? I think most of us can stand anything for sixty seconds. That is not a very long time.

I do not believe Joseph was being asked to endure his suffering for just sixty seconds. What he was asked to do was place the meaning and purpose behind his suffering into a new point of view—an eternal perspective. The Lord was essentially inviting Joseph to place his imprisonment upon the eternal time line or continuum of his life and in relationship to God and His Only Begotten Son. He was given a new clock from which he could tell a new time.

The Lord was not minimizing or belittling Joseph's suffering. He was not telling him to simply think of something else, or to think of more pleasant things. He was not asking him to forget about himself and his loved ones. He was not telling Joseph to calm down or chill out. He was not telling him that this was not a big deal. He was not telling him that he was making a mountain out of a molehill.

Instead, the Lord acknowledged the Prophet's suffering, and then reminded Joseph of the purpose of such suffering and pain. He taught him that those things he was experiencing, though daunting, were not his eternal destiny. There was more to his life, his calling, and his relationship to the Almighty than the privations of that cramped jail cell.

Of course Joseph was worried about his loved ones who were being subjected to ridicule, harassment, assaults, and even death. But those agonies would not last forever. His suffering would not last forever. But there were critical things that the experience in Liberty Jail taught Joseph about himself, about the Lord, and about their relationship. Joseph, in turn, teaches us.

Mortality is not an easy or momentary proposition. There are periods of pain and grief that we are called on to endure, but they do not last for an eternity. They do not hang over us without some respite. We are not doomed or damned by having to persevere through moments, hours, weeks, and even years of trials. Nor are we left alone. We are not left without answers. We are not left without our Lord.

During tough times, time does appear to stop. We feel like we have lost our reference point. We feel disoriented. We focus on only the "now" of our suffering and afflictions. That is understandable. That is nothing to be ashamed of or embarrassed about. It is not easy to disregard what is hurting us or ignore who is hurting us. We want the pain to stop. Now.

Most of the time it doesn't. At least, not instantaneously. But we, like Joseph, can still be comforted and taught and become more perfected in our knowledge of who we are and who He is.

More often than not, trials and tribulations are something to go through and carry. We do not often escape or elude them. We are required to endure. But the Lord promises, "And then, if thou endure it well, God shall exalt thee on high; thou shalt triumph over all thy foes" (D&C 121:8). The time will ultimately come when "God shall wipe away all tears from [our] eyes; and there shall be no more death, neither sorrow, nor crying, neither shall there be any more pain" (Revelation 21:4). But that is not now. For now, in mortality, we are to endure our afflictions patiently.

How are we expected to endure things well? What does that mean to us? Where do we turn for guidance and strength?

When my father told me that I would never walk or run like the other children, his words made me sad and brought me to tears. It was painful to realize that I simply could not do certain things. But my father did not leave me alone in my fear. When I longed to accomplish my mission and live my life, even with a severe physical

By a swimming pool, August 1962.

disability, my father reminded me of the things I could do. He told me of my strengths. He assured me that I was loved. He told me he would remain close and watch me grow.

The copy of *Look* magazine chronicled photographs of a man who had faced his own challenges and rose above them in order to help others during perilous and frightening times. My father gave me an exemplar to follow. He gave me a hero. He gave me hope. And he gave me a plan that would help me succeed.

Likewise, there is a plan for all of us. It is a plan that will help us not only endure every trial and every adversity no matter how short or how prolonged, but it is also a plan that helps us endure them well.

At the age of four I met my hero. But I had to wait until I was twelve to meet my God.

CHAPTER TWO

"IN THE WORLD YE SHALL HAVE TRIBULATION"

By the time I was twelve years old my body resembled a pretzel. My spine was twisted and contorted into a severe S-curve. My doctors called it scoliosis—a curvature of my spinal column. Because my lungs were being compressed and breathing was difficult, I could not sit for long periods of time in my wheelchair. Due to lack of physical activity, I gained quite a bit of weight in the ensuing years. I weighed more than 150 pounds, and that was a prescription for an impending disaster.

Something needed to be done, but there were very few options. As a temporary stopgap to stave off my growing discomfort and pain, my physicians in Cleveland, Ohio, demanded that I wear a rigid corset, which was annoying beyond belief. Since I sat in my wheelchair in a way that already pitched my upper body forward, the stays of the corset would dig into my thighs and back. Each morning when my mother cinched the corset into place, I would plead for her not to pull the straps too tightly so that it would not hurt so much.

With my sister Judy, the summer prior to my spinal fusion operation. I was twelve years old.

She hated having to hurt me. Even at that age, I knew how hard it was for her to cinch up those stays. My curved spine was causing both of us a lot of pain.

We all knew that the corset was not arresting the curvature of my spine. The only remedy for straightening my spine was surgery, and that was a hard reality for me to accept. The doctors called the operation a spinal fusion. But what that meant was that my spine would be straightened and lengthened by the insertion of a long metal rod that would be reinforced and buttressed by—believe it or not—horse bone. I would have to spend six months in a spica hip cast.

The cast would extend from the back of my skull down to my knees and would enclose my shoulders, chest, stomach, hips, and thighs. The only openings would be openings for my arms and to allow for my bodily functions. Additionally, there would be an eighteen-inch rod to keep my knees separated. To me, the prospect of such surgery sounded like a punishment introduced in the Middle Ages.

Additionally, I would have to lie in this froglike position, completely immobilized, and would not be able to sit upright for six whole months. That is a long time, especially for a twelve-year-old who was so busy being a boy and playing with his brother, Billy, and sister Judy that he seldom saw himself as different or disabled.

It was a frightening prospect. What made it even more terrifying was the fact that no child in America as disabled as I was had ever undergone this radical operation, and no one with such diminished lung capacity as mine had ever survived it. In order to evaluate my chances of survival, I had to breathe repeatedly into a machine prior to the surgery to demonstrate to my doctors that I had the strength to take a deep breath. Those tests had not gone well. In fact, the results caused more worry than they provided promise, and my parents were told there was only a fifty percent chance that I would wake up from the surgery.

But the results did not discourage my doctors to the degree that surgery was taken off the table as an option to save my life. We reached a conclusion: surgery was the only remaining hope. The procedure was scheduled for July 1968.

As we were riding home from that last doctor's appointment, my father said to me, "Son, we have to do this. This is the best choice we have to lengthen and save your life. If we continue what we are doing, you will live a short and painful life."

That is a lot to absorb, especially when you are in the seventh grade. I did not want to think of life-altering experiences. I was excited about going to a new school and continuing to follow baseball and meeting new girls. In many respects, I was just like any other seventh grader. I did not know just how risky the operation would be.

The night before surgery, I had to say good-bye to my mother and father. I could see the concern on their faces and feel the worry in their hearts. I remember my mother saying, "I am sorry you have to go through this. If I could go through it for you I would, but

I can't. You have to have faith and be our brave boy. God has not brought you this far to fail. Try to get some sleep, and we will see you in the morning."

And then they left. I was alone in the dark of a Cleveland hospital with only my fears.

An orderly came in and shaved my entire body. He was very nice, but I felt even more afraid and vulnerable after he left. I think I might have been the loneliest boy in America that night in 1968.

But I was not left alone. There was someone worried about me and concerned about me. There was Someone watching over me.

My mother could not teach me how to walk or how to ride a bicycle. But she had taught me something even more important; she had taught me how to pray without kneeling. Our family had some experience with rote prayers, but Mother had taught me that I should not always say the same prayer in the same way to Heavenly Father, and she encouraged me to be frank about my fears and concerns as I spoke to Him. But more importantly, she taught me to believe that God answers prayers.

So on that hot July night in Cleveland, Ohio, I offered a simple petition. The man in the bed next to mine had been sleeping for hours, and I said, "God, if everything is going to be alright tomorrow, would you please make the man lying in the bed next to me cough or turn over?" And then I ended my prayer.

I knew I was asking a lot because my roommate had been unconscious for hours. He had not made a single movement or gesture. He had not turned. He had not coughed or groaned.

I testify to you that within ten seconds after I uttered my simple prayer, the man who had been in a semi-coma in the bed next to me sat bolt upright in his bed.

He was fully awake!

He turned his body and faced me. And then he said, "Stevie, if you need anything during the night, just let me know. I am here for you."

Then he immediately fell back to sleep.

I had received my answer.

I learned that night that God knew my name. That God was aware of my life and that He was involved in my life. He was concerned about me, just as my earthly parents were. He was there for me, just as my earthly parents were. He loved me, just as my earthly parents did.

I was alone. But I wasn't.

I felt as though I had been forgotten. But I wasn't.

I felt as though I had been forsaken. But I wasn't.

God was on my side.

God was at my side.

Indeed, I was His child.

I was in His care.

I was in His arms.

I had faith that He would be with me in the operating room the next morning. I had faith that I would live. I had faith that I would see my parents again. I had faith that I would regain my health.

I could not envision the end. I could not experience everything beforehand. But I had the faith that I could press forward. I could hope and I could believe and I could have faith for a better tomorrow.

<hr />

Of course I would still have to submit to the operation. My spine was not miraculously or painlessly straightened by an angel. There would be much pain and discomfort in my immediate future. I would not be spared the exquisite agony of having my crooked spine fused and straightened through a six-hour operation. But that is not the importance of the answer to my simple prayer.

The answer was that I did not have to go through this ordeal—any of it—alone. Even though my parents would not be in the surgical suite, there would be Someone watching over me.

During His mortal ministry, Jesus explained to His disciples, "In the world ye shall have tribulation: but be of good cheer; I have overcome the world" (John 16:33).

Somehow, many of us believe that Jesus was talking generally and not specifically. Somehow we want to believe that He was talking only to them and not to us.

But I know He was talking to us. All of us. He was talking to both you and me.

He did not say that in the world we *might* or *may have* tribulation. He said that we *shall* or *will*. This means we *must* experience tribulation.

None of us can escape trials, tribulation, and sorrow. Not one of us.

We hope we can. We think we can. We are sometimes even sure we can. But that is not what He said.

Trials and tribulation are a necessary part of life on this earth. It is an irrefutable, unequivocal fact of our mortal lives that adversity is to play an integral role. That is a given. Of course we all wish that we could escape heartbreak and agony. We cannot. We are not supposed to. Adversity is our universal affliction. It happens to each one of us, and often it happens when we least expect it. Most of the time it happens more than once. And it always causes us physical or emotional or spiritual anguish.

Adversity also consumes us; when it comes, it is very difficult to think of anything else. It is overwhelming. It has a great deal of power over what we think about and how we feel. Tribulation visits us wherever we live and wherever we work. It does not matter how young or how old we are. It does not matter how much we know or how much we earn. It does not matter how learned or wise we are or how many degrees we have obtained. It does not matter if we have faced previous challenges or overcome earlier hurdles throughout our lives.

Trials and tests seem to accompany us. Sometimes we cannot see them coming, and they arrive abruptly. Sometimes they linger. They are life's unwelcome guests.

When we are facing and dealing with trials, we often feel as though the peace and serenity of our lives will never return.

Trials come to both the strong and the weak. They find us. There is no disputing that.

Adversity is a necessary part of the plan of salvation. It is more of a question of how you and I will respond when adversity or sorrow enters our lives. What choices will we make? Where will we turn for answers? Where will we look for relief?

We sometimes forget that Jesus faced trials. And those trials did not occur only during the last critical and agonizing hours of His earthly life. The challenges He faced were frequent and recurring. They were part of His life. He did not escape them. He did not avoid them. What He did is pass through them. Most important, He overcame them.

The trials began in the humble circumstances of His birth, which were the epitome of privation and lowliness. They continued in Herod's attempt to kill Him. At the beginning of His ministry, following His forty-day fast, He was tempted in the wilderness by Satan (Matthew 4:1–11). He was offered nourishment and worldly power if He would succumb to the devil's self-serving, malevolent designs, which had already been rejected by two-thirds of the spirits in the premortal world.

The Jews attempted to stone Him after He declared Himself at the synagogue as the Messiah (John 10:23–39). Later, three of the eleven disciples—Peter, James, and John—slept in the olive orchard despite His admonition that they "watch and pray" (Matthew 26:41; Mark 14:38) as He began His lonely descent into the despair and agony of Gethsemane.

Even more galling was the blatant betrayal from one of His closest confidants, Judas, who rushed out of the upper room of the Last Supper to concoct the specious charges that the Sanhedrin leveled against Jesus, and who led the bloodthirsty Jewish mob into the Garden to seize the Innocent One. Astonishingly, Peter—for reasons that are still not entirely understood—issued three separate denials when he was questioned concerning his knowledge of and relationship with Jesus (Matthew 26:69–75; Mark 14:66–72; Luke 22:54–62; John 18:15–27).

So what is the purpose of adversity? Why is it all around us? What is its role in our lives? Why must we go through such hard, trying times? Why is adversity such a central part of the plan of salvation? What do sadness, sorrow, and grief have to do with the plan of happiness, as Alma described it (Alma 42:8)?

The Lord is clear that the purpose of trials is meant to test our faith in Him and our obedience to His commandments. "We will prove them herewith," He said, "to see if they will do all things whatsoever the Lord their God shall command them" (Abraham 3:25).

Is it possible to be happy during bad times or sad times?

Of course, there is no expectation that adversity and affliction will bring an immediate smile to our faces or laughter into our lives. That is simply illogical, unrealistic, and, in most circumstances, impossible. Adversity brings tears, pain, uncertainty, anxiety, fear, anger, frustration, depression, grief, and mourning.

Yet it is important to note that the Savior stated, "These things I have spoken unto you, that in *me* ye might have peace. In the world ye shall have tribulation: but be of good cheer; *I* have overcome the world" (John 16:33; emphasis added).

When Jesus promised that trials and tribulations would be part of our lives, He did not exhort us to celebrate them or to take them lightly. Instead, He draws our attention to them—and to Him. That is a very important connection that we too often forget when we are going through difficult times in our lives.

He declares that it is through Him that we can find peace in the midst of affliction and troubles.

He then says that we should "be of good cheer" because He has overcome the world. But being of good cheer does not necessarily mean being jolly or silly or giddy during our tough times. There is little that is fun or funny about the tragedies we are asked to endure.

So what exactly does "good cheer" mean? To understand, we need look no further than the next phrase: We can be of good cheer *because He overcame the world.* Consequently, I believe being of good cheer means focusing on His power and His love. We may approach, pass through, endure, and, yes, even overcome our challenges by focusing on Christ.

It is His power that overcame this life, this world, and even death. Why did He do it? Why did He overcome? Because He loves us. He will see us through the tough days and challenges. He has promised us that. And He does not break His promises. Not ever.

He is our Savior, our Friend, and our Advocate. He is our promise keeper.

As a result, the cheerfulness that you and I are encouraged to exemplify during difficult times is a quiet, serene confidence that all is well or that all will be made well because we are His followers and the sheep of His fold. We have not been forgotten or abandoned.

Jesus Christ is therefore both the Good News and the Good Cheer contained in and defined by His gospel.

As Alma observes in Alma 7:11–12:

> And he shall go forth, suffering pains and afflictions and temptations of every kind; and this that the word might be fulfilled which saith he will take upon him the pains and the sicknesses of his people.
>
> And he will take upon him death, that he may loose the bands of death which bind his people; and he will take upon him their infirmities, that his bowels may be filled with mercy, according to the flesh, that he may know according to the flesh how to succor his people according to their infirmities.

In an unfathomable way, Jesus, while in the Garden, took upon Himself every pain, every affliction, every temptation, every doubt, every disappointment, every loss, every grief, every illness, every disease, and every agony that anyone has experienced or will experience in this life. It is difficult to comprehend it all!

Jacob reaffirms this truth:

> And he cometh into the world that he may save all men if they will hearken unto his voice; for behold, he suffereth the pains of all men, yea, the pains of every living creature, both men, women, and children, who belong to the family of Adam. (2 Nephi 9:21)

Jesus suffered not only for our sins, but He also suffered the pains of every man, woman, and child. No one is excluded from His love and mercy. No one is left out. No one is abandoned. No one is forsaken. No one is ignored. No one is forgotten. No one is left alone to suffer. No one.

The Atonement is as intimate as it is infinite. In some

incomprehensible way, Jesus knows and understands everything about us. He understands us perfectly. He knows what we are asked to live with, experience, and endure.

In some inexplicable way, Jesus has already faced our fears and cried our tears.

Consequently, Jesus asks us to pass through nothing which He Himself has not already experienced, and, more important, nothing which He hasn't already overcome for us.

No matter how difficult or painful our adversity, Jesus remains the Christ. He still loves us. His peace can still envelop us, and we can still access His love. We can still have confidence and hope and faith and love that no matter what is asked of us in this life, comfort and peace come by and through Him. He stands firm. He has not gone anywhere.

He is the source and the light of truth, comfort, and good cheer. So the answer to the question of how we can maintain good cheer during trials is that we can have confidence that Jesus is there for us and will help us through. Jesus is *good cheer*. We can trust that He will give us the strength to endure.

He will never let us down. He never tires of listening to and loving us during the times when we feel alone and sorrowful.

Adversity comes, but so does He!

That is why we can have confidence and hope—He is there to help us through our trials. That is the promise. That is the truth. He sees us through the dark times and shows us the way through His light, life, and love.

As He promised both then and now to all of us, "Be of good cheer, little children; for I am in your midst, and I have not forsaken you" (D&C 61:36).

Again He says, "Be of good cheer, for I will lead you along. The kingdom is yours and the blessings thereof are yours, and the riches of eternity are yours" (D&C 78:18).

This is not an understanding I had at age twelve when confronted with the reality of my physical condition. What I did understand at that point was that God knew me, that He knew my name, and that He would not abandon me. My testimony of these additional truths would not fully develop for several more years.

———⟨∙⟩———

I have discovered that the Lord often meets our needs and comforts us through other human beings. And when I awakened from my six-hour spinal surgery, I saw a beautiful, smiling face. My mom's face. When I saw her, I knew I had lived through the surgery. I had survived. My prayer, and the answer to it, had given me the confidence and hope that I needed to face the next day and the next months. I focused on her face and her faith.

I remember thinking it was a little strange that my father was holding on to her so tightly in the recovery room. Later I learned that she had nearly fainted when she saw me lying in the bed of dried blood that I had lost during the ordeal. He was holding her so she wouldn't collapse. She and I were both in shock about what I had passed through.

But she was focused on me. And I was focused on her radiant smile, which was always there. Her smile and her constant care and love sustained me then and would be my strength in the years to come.

My spine was straightened. My heart was comforted. My pain was bearable. And because of the answer I received from my prayer and the constant love lavished on me by my mother, my life became more cheerful.

CHAPTER THREE

"WE DO NOT DOUBT OUR MOTHERS KNEW IT"

The first memory of my life was not about being frustrated or sad about the fact that I was unable to stand or walk. My first memory did not occur in some doctor's chilly office or lonely hospital room. I do not remember being discouraged during those early years over my limitations.

My first memory is of being kissed—a lot—by my mother. I remember those kisses and how much she loved me. What a tremendous blessing and message I received from her.

No one should ever underestimate the profound power of a mother's love. Not ever. In her presence:

I felt loved.

I felt appreciated.

I felt nurtured.

I felt adored.

I felt safe.

I felt secure.

My mother, Mildred Mikita,
approximately age twenty-eight.

In her arms, I experienced the priceless gift of a mother's love.

I can say that the foundation of my faith and the cornerstone of my testimony are the result of my mother's love. It is as simple as that. Without her love, I would never have come to know His love. Without her at my side during trial after trial, I would not have approached my life with a muscle disease with as much optimism, resolve, and resilience as I have.

She set both the standard and the rhythm of my life. It was she who taught me to believe there is purpose in trials. She helped me to interpret the meaning of the good times and the bad. Surely, there would be both. Life was not comprised of only victories and triumphs. We would suffer setbacks and losses. We would laugh together and cry together. We would grieve and celebrate.

My mother made up for that which I lacked. Her love filled the gaps. Her love was my strength. Though we were not yet members of The Church of Jesus Christ of Latter-day Saints, with the additional understanding that the gospel would bring, her implicit faith in God inspired me and instructed me.

She was the one who lifted me out of my crib, dressed me, fed me, and nurtured me every day. But unlike most mothers, she continued this routine for many years until I became too heavy and her back became too weak to allow her to continue. But she still did it. Every day. Every year.

She was the first person who greeted me in the morning and the last person who told me goodnight for the first eighteen years of my life. What is even more compelling is that she would also turn me over from one side to another three or four times each and every night.

She did it all, and without a single complaint. She did it gladly and cheerfully. I was never made to feel that I was a burden. Rather, I was her son, and she viewed the service she gave to me as a gift and a privilege.

My doctors were always quick to offer their view of how sad, how frustrated, how abbreviated, and how depressing my life would be. Their diagnoses and prognoses of a life of hopelessness came from textbooks. But their analyses of my muscle disease—Spinal Muscular Atrophy—discounted one stunning element, one undeniable factor that made it possible for me to live a life full of meaning and resolve: my mother's love.

Mother countered the doctors' stark, clinical observations with steely determination and a profound faith that all would be well. I see it so clearly now; there was a reason why God had sent me to her.

She was resolved to find out why I had been born with this disability and then, with His help, discover how to implement His plan for me as best and as effectively as she could. Those who saw only the drudgery of providing for my needs discounted the power of her faith and love.

In the first couple of years of my life, Mother spent many hours in mighty prayer seeking for guidance. She searched for answers, and her heart was open to those answers. She knew she could not raise a special needs child without help—divine help.

It was not easy, and she was plagued by bouts of depression. One day there was a knock at the door. Two LDS missionaries introduced themselves as representatives of Jesus Christ. I was only three years old and playing on the floor, and Mother explained to her visitors that she was distressed over my inability to walk.

When Mother told them that my name was John Stephen, one of the missionaries said, "That is a beautiful name. John was one of Jesus' disciples, and Stephen was martyred for standing up for his beliefs in Christ's divinity."

Mother was moved to tears by those simple but insightful comments.

My parents were practicing Episcopalians, but Mother offered money to the two young men. The missionaries respectfully declined the gift and explained that they did not accept money for their service. They asked if they could visit her again, and she accepted.

Later that night, after Mother explained to my father who her visitors were, he told her that he did not approve of Mormons and declared that they were happy being Episcopalians. My mother had belonged to the Serbian Orthodox Church and my father had belonged to the Russian Orthodox Church; they had decided to join the Episcopal Church after they were married as a religious compromise. My father felt that he had sacrificed enough by leaving his boyhood traditions. However, Mother did not forget her visitors, and it would not be our only encounter with The Church of Jesus Christ of Latter-day Saints.

All mothers make a difference. Mothers are indispensable to the lives, testimonies, development, and faith of their children.

Mothers matter.

My mother taught me the meaning of the words bravery, resiliency, endurance, faith, tenacity, and gratitude. All of those attributes are conveyed to a child by a mother through one process: *nurturing*. To nurture means to train, to protect, to cultivate, to instill, and to propagate in another certain principles and beliefs (see "The Family: A Proclamation to the World," 102).

My mother taught me how to pray. She taught me when to pray and what to pray for. She discouraged her children from saying rote prayers. Instead, she encouraged all of us to speak to God with reverence and to share our feelings and our fears. She urged us to express our gratitude for the good things of our lives. She knew intuitively from whom all blessings flow, and she was determined to instill that understanding into each of us.

But besides teaching me how to pray, my mother taught me how to fight. She taught me how to prepare for battle and how to endure pain and terror. During my many hospitalizations, I would sometimes want to surrender. But her response was always the same: "Every day is a new fight. That is part of your life. That is part of living with a disability. You must not get discouraged. Life sometimes is unfair, but God loves you and I love you. He has not brought you this far to fail. This hospitalization or this ordeal will help us take better care of you. It will help extend your life so that you can achieve those things that you are meant to do in this life."

I held to her words when I was facing tough times and overcoming adversity. She was constantly reminding me who I was, how much I was loved, and what she and I were capable of enduring because of what we had already overcome.

My mother also taught me the importance of being a good

spiritual historian so that I would not forget what I had endured. That is part of what a mother is. Mothers remember what their children have gone through. They remember what their children have done. They remember what they have said. They remember what they needed and when they needed it. Mothers simply remember.

If we are to endure and learn from the difficult moments in our lives, we must remember where we have been. In doing so, we acquire the hope and faith that we can keep on going, no matter the challenge and no matter how formidable the foe.

In the face of each new challenge in my affliction, my mother would remind me of previous trials that we had endured together and overcome. She would recite the lessons of faith and perseverance that we had learned. She would recall the instances and moments that God had stretched forth His hand to heal, comfort, and deliver me. She remembered the lessons of her faith and the beginnings of mine.

These are some of the lessons that my mother taught me about adversity: Adversity is a part of my life and your life and your children's lives. But we are not left alone to contend with, pass through, or overcome these trials. We are not alone.

Her outlook, which became mine as well, is that we have help. Powerful help. Consistent help. Constant help. One of the primary answers to adversity is that God blesses us with mothers to teach, love, and nurture us through the difficult experiences of our lives on earth. God enlists mothers to help His children learn about Him and to rely on Him in mortality. In this, they are ministering angels to us.

I came to understand that my life could be successfully lived without strong muscles. But I could not have survived without my strong mother.

There was once a fierce warrior who recognized the undeniable importance and influence of a mother's love. His name was Helaman. He understood war and peace. He understood courage and determination. He understood young bravery and valor. Most important, he understood the role that mothers play in teaching their children about the meaning of life and the answers to adversity.

Speaking of the remarkable young warriors he commanded in battle, Helaman states:

> And now I say unto you, my beloved brother Moroni, that never had I seen so great courage, nay, not amongst all the Nephites.
>
> For as I had ever called them my sons (for they were all of them very young) even so they said unto me: Father, behold our God is with us, and he will not suffer that we should fall; then let us go forth; we would not slay our brethren if they would let us alone; therefore let us go, lest they should overpower the army of Antipus.
>
> Now they never had fought, yet they did not fear death; and they did think more upon the liberty of their fathers than they did upon their lives; yea, they had been taught by their mothers, that if they did not doubt, God would deliver them.
>
> And they rehearsed unto me the words of their mothers, saying: We do not doubt our mothers knew it. (Alma 56:45–48)

So where did these brave souls, these young warriors, learn to confront death without fear? They were taught by their mothers.

Where did they learn that God was with them? From their mothers.

How was it that they did not fear death? Their fearlessness came from the teachings of their mothers.

Why is it that they prized liberty above their own safety? Their mothers had instilled in them a love of freedom, liberty, and independence.

How is it that these young men did not doubt? Their mothers had raised them to have faith and not doubt in the power of God to love and protect them when facing overwhelming odds.

How did Helaman know of the character and the faith of his fledgling army? How did he conclude that they were ready to meet their enemies? These young men must have told Helaman the lessons they remembered being taught by their respective mothers.

These young men were protected by more than armor, muscle, training, and valor. They were armored with and shielded by their mothers' love. They were ready to fight for a great cause because their mothers had prepared them to cherish that cause.

But it was not just one battle that these warriors would have to fight. Many who read this account focus on the miracle that every single stripling warrior survived. That is certainly a testament to their faith and righteousness.

But the story of this miracle army did not end with a single victory. The story is one of faith, but also one of enduring to the end.

It is accurate that these faithful freedom fighters did escape death. But that does not mean that they were free of adversity for the remainder of their lives. Many challenges remained for all of them. Given the time and place where they lived, they must have endured trying moments and difficult days. Adversity did not likely visit them only when they were young and strong. Their mothers had not prepared them for just one experience with adversity. They had prepared their sons to live with faith for the rest of their lives.

Helaman writes:

And it came to pass that there were two hundred, out of my two thousand and sixty, who had fainted because of the loss of blood; nevertheless, according to the goodness of God, and to our great astonishment, and also the joy of our whole army, there was not one soul of them who did perish; yea, and *neither was there one soul among them who had not received many wounds.*

And now, their preservation was astonishing to our whole army, yea, that they should be spared while there was a thousand of our brethren who were slain. And we do justly ascribe it to the miraculous power of God, because of their exceeding faith in that which they had been taught to believe—that there was a just God, and whosoever did not doubt, that they should be preserved by his marvelous power.

Now this was the faith of these of whom I have spoken; they are young, and their minds are firm, and they do put their trust in God continually. (Alma 57:25–27; emphasis added)

None of them was spared from receiving "many wounds." One can only imagine the severity of these wounds when considering the primitive weapons used in this battle.

Doubtless, these young warriors would rely upon the faith taught to them by their mothers throughout their lives in dealing with their postwar injuries and disabilities. Their lives were never the same; but their faith was firm, despite their many wounds.

I am convinced that they could not have survived those years after the battle if they had not learned that adversity is not a one-time experience. Adversity happens to all of us. It typically lasts more than one day and happens more than once during a lifetime.

But you and I are not left alone. Mothers help us understand why we must pass through such painful and traumatic experiences. They remind us in whom we can trust. They tell us in whom we can place our confidence. They ask us to draw upon previous experiences. Mothers ready us for adversity. Mothers also ready us for the answers to adversity. They often direct our attention heavenward. They ask us to have faith. They join us in mighty prayer to overcome the enemies and opponents that try to defeat us and cause us to doubt that God is watching us as He watched over the young stripling army of Helaman.

Mothers give us more than weapons and shields and swords. They give us perspective. They give us pause to consider where we have been, what we are doing, and where we are going. Mothers remember single battles and lifelong battles. They give us their undivided attention when we need it most. Mothers notice our scars, both visible and invisible.

Mothers prepare us to answer adversity's call and face the trials of life. They prepare our souls to receive answers and to open our hearts to gain a broader perspective when we lose our way and forget who we are. Mothers are there to cheer us on and to pray for our safe return.

My mother taught me all these things, not in dramatic or grand ways, but in the quiet, private moments we spent together. Much of what I know about confronting and enduring adversity I learned as I held my mother's hand as she sat by my bedside hour after hour, day after day, week after week. There was no one watching. Well, at least, no one we could see with our eyes.

Because most of my hospitalizations took place in Cleveland,

Ohio, Mother spent her nights alone at a nearby hotel. Even when she was at the hospital, there was no one around to give her a break. My siblings were at home—three hours away. Dad was attending to his patients and could only visit on weekends.

Even her meals were fleeting. She would run downstairs to the hospital cafeteria and quickly grab a salad or a cup of soup. She never complained about the food or the lack of company. These were the days where there were no text messages, cell phones, or computers. She could talk to Dad and my brother and sisters only during brief telephone conversations from my room.

During the summer of 1968, when I was undergoing my spinal fusion and recuperation from the surgery, there was a great deal of racial unrest in our country, especially in larger cities, such as Cleveland. Riots broke out between the African-American population in Cleveland and the police. To control the growing tensions, the National Guard was eventually deployed.

Mother would report on the number of tanks and other armored vehicles that were moving around below the window of my room at the University Hospital. Curfews were issued. The streets were empty. Each night during that summer, she left my hospital room alone but without fear and without complaint.

If she felt insecure and unprotected as she walked through a dimly lit parking lot and past army tanks and police barricades, she never said anything about it to me. She was more concerned about my survival than her own.

Hospital visiting hours were strictly enforced, and she didn't want to leave me each night at eight o'clock when visiting hours ended. She knew how desperately I relied on her strength—sometimes from one moment to the next. Each night, she would remind me of what we had learned and where we were going. We would both shed tears as she departed.

We had gotten through one more day—together. We had won one more battle—together. I was still alive.

She never left my presence without offering a prayer of thanksgiving and a petition for guidance and direction. I knew she was grateful to be a wife, a mother, and a child of God because I heard her say so in her prayers. I knew she loved God and her family and the Church because I heard her say so in her prayers. There was no doubt: she understood her mission; she knew what to do and how to do it. She had her priorities straight, and she knew where to turn for refuge and rescue.

When I think of her selfless sacrifice and service, I am humbled beyond words. She never complained. I was her son, and she was my mother. She stood by me through every challenge and ordeal. She soothed me in my suffering.

––––⊶⊷––––

At the age of twelve, I began to realize what a gift I had received in my mother. I recognized and was aware of what she was giving up to sit beside me and support me. She was a physician's wife. She had a beautiful home. She drove a nice car. But none of that mattered. It never had.

We were bonded in a remarkable way. I felt sorry for her for having to leave me each night. Just as she worried about me, I worried about her. I worried about her safety. I worried about being a burden. I worried about her being tired. I worried about her missing Dad and my siblings—Carole, Billy, and Judy—and all of the time she was spending away from the rest of the family. And I worried about her worrying about me.

I wanted to get better for both of us. She deserved so much

Mildred Mikita.

happiness and peace. We had both been through so much together. I empathized for her and with her.

I learned a lot about life and adversity that summer of 1968. I learned about suffering and pain. I learned about faith. I learned about the power of prayer. But I also learned about compassion and the gift of motherhood. That is how I felt toward my mother as she watched and waited and prayed by my side.

Speaking of the priceless gift of motherhood, President Thomas S. Monson has written:

> The holy scriptures, the pages of history are replete with tender, moving, convincing accounts of "mother loved." One, however, stands out supreme, above and beyond any other. The place is Jerusalem, the period known as the Meridian of Time. Assembled is a throng of Roman

soldiers. Their helmets signify their loyalty to Caesar, their
shields bear his emblem, their spears are crowned by Roman
eagles. Assembled also are natives to the land of Jerusalem.
Faded into the still night, and gone forever are the militant
and rowdy cries, "Crucify him, crucify him."

The hour has come. The personal earthly ministry of
the Son of God moves swiftly to its dramatic conclusion. A
certain loneliness is here. . . . There remained yet a few faithful followers. From his tortured position on the cruel cross,
he sees his mother and the disciple whom he loved standing
by. He speaks: ". . . woman, behold thy son! Then saith he
to the disciple, Behold thy mother! . . ." (John 19:26–27.)

From that awful night when time stood still, when the
earth did quake and great mountains were brought down—
yes, through the annals of history, over the centuries of years
and beyond the span of time, there echoes his simple yet
divine words, "Behold thy mother!" . . .

May each of us treasure this truth; one cannot forget
mother and remember God. One cannot remember mother
and forget God. Why? Because these two sacred persons,
God and mother, partners in creation, in love, in sacrifice,
in service, are as one. (Monson, "'Behold Thy Mother,'"
31–32)

It would be impossible for me to exaggerate the blessing my
mother has been in my life. Several years ago, I reflected on the relationship we enjoyed:

As she did every evening before tucking me into bed
and saying goodnight, Mother would switch on the night-
light near the door to comfort me during her temporary

absence. Realizing instinctively that this night would last considerably longer than other nights, Mother has provided me with a host of night-lights to guide and sustain me until we meet again and embrace each other forevermore.

When the distraught physicians predicted that I would tarry no longer than two years with her, they had obviously overlooked the angelic ministrant who held me so fervently and securely in her arms and quietly but stubbornly refused to obey their prognosis of resigned death. Mother instead filled me with her divine prescription of faith, hope, and love, which has proven to be more reliable than any mortal muscle could ever be. She injected me with a vision of life, which overflowed with challenging possibilities that would combine unspeakable joy to me and glory to God.

Among her teachings were these calming assurances:

"Inseparable brothers, Joseph and Hyrum; Billy and Stevie."

"The only true Church."

"Dad, we've got the best kids in the world!"

"God lives."

"Don't be afraid; Mommy's here."

"Jesus is the Christ."

"I am so proud of you kids; you give me too much credit."

"Don't cry, punky puss. God hasn't brought you this far to fail."

"I'm not afraid to die. I have been too blessed."

Is it any wonder that I revere her and credit her with instilling in me the hope and resiliency that have sustained me to this point in my life? Her reflections on our premortal yesterdays have always

Mildred Mikita, approximately 1970.

eased the harshness of my mortal tomorrows. Of equal magnitude are her serene and sober discourses on the Garden and the Grove. I will be eternally grateful to her for having instilled in me her faith in the wonder of the empty tomb and the blessings of latter-day temples.

So I cannot repay my mother. Can anyone? There is no price for a mother's everlasting love. I can only give thanks and honor her by living the principles she taught me and by loving others as she loved me.

CHAPTER FOUR

※◁IIIᘲ⌂ᕽIIIᐒ◁

"BOW DOWN
THINE EAR,
O LORD"

To say that the months immediately following my spinal fusion were difficult would be an understatement. My spine was nice and straight, but my life was turned upside down by a new trial. Because of the cast I wore, I felt as though I was the victim of a science project gone terribly awry. I was surrounded by a shell of plaster that covered two-thirds of my body. I resembled a white turtle!

But there was nothing funny about my new way of life. The pain from my spine was gone, but the frustration and discomfort of my life inside this plaster prison was positively maddening.

I could not sit up.

I could not drive my wheelchair.

I had lost a lot of my freedom.

I had lost a lot of my independence.

I had lost a lot of my privacy.

Before my spinal fusion, I had lived a very active and somewhat normal boyhood existence.

I had been happy, carefree, and active.

Now I could not attend school.

I could not play all of the games that my creative brother, Billy, had designed so we could play together on our driveway or on the street.

I could not go on car rides, or out to restaurants, or attend sporting events.

I could not go to the movies or shopping with my family, even though Pittsburgh was only forty miles away.

My life had been placed on hold—for at least the next six months.

Everything that I used to do either had to be postponed or done in a different way. If I wanted to watch television, I had to wear prism glasses, which contained mirrors that would reflect the images from the television.

I could still eat, but I had to chew very carefully.

None of these challenges compared to the physical discomfort of living inside the cast. It caused me chronic itchiness. It seemed that there was always a new itch that no one could reach. I detested having to take sponge baths, and I felt as if my hair could never be washed thoroughly. I felt unkempt and dirty.

Getting ready in the morning took two hours—but it seemed like forever.

Although I could not attend school with my fellow classmates and enjoy the beginning months of the seventh grade, I still participated through an intercom system that my parents provided to the school and which could be transferred from class to class, allowing me to listen to every class from home. If I wanted to participate by asking or answering a question, I would simply hit a button on my receiver and my classmates and teachers would hear my voice over the intercom.

So that I could attend school from home and take notes for class, I was rotated every morning and suspended face down over the side of a hospital gurney. Then, so my head would not fall forward, a restraining strap was tied around my forehead and attached to the back of the cast.

My new life in the cast was emotionally difficult as well. I was missing out on a lot of the sociality of middle school. I was not only "the boy in the shell," I was also "the voice in the box." Without the companionship of my schoolmates, I was lonely and frustrated. I felt invisible.

I also felt isolated from my family. Our family room was ostensibly converted into a studio apartment. It was where I spent all of my time and where I would spend the next six months of my life. That room was where I had all of my meals, slept, listened to school, and watched television. I shared the space with my caregiver, Ronnie Linton, a man from Jamaica who my parents had hired to help me with my needs. He was a very short but physically powerful man who was able to manipulate my body and the heavy cast. Though we were together for eighteen months, we were never anything more than associates in a difficult situation.

It was particularly frustrating to realize how life was moving along for others while I was going through this particular trial. Knowing how close I was to normalcy was particularly galling. Having people just in the next room or seeing them on the television or talking to them on the telephone or over the intercom made me long even more to live as others lived. Even a return to my previous life—outside the confinement of that room—was something I dreamed about.

Though I knew I was loved, I was still unhappy and depressed. Looking back, I suppose I shouldn't have expected anything else. While going through adversity, it is altogether natural to feel lonely, isolated, and oppressed. It was hard for me to focus on anything beyond my confinement. That reality robbed me of my energy and diminished my will to fight. I often felt very much as though I had been chosen to walk alone—without assistance, without help, and without deliverance. I was impatient and tired of waiting for my recovery. I wanted to rejoin life and return to happy times. I wanted the pain and the grief to stop.

I thought that my six-month sojourn in the wilderness with my cross of plaster would end as soon as it was sawed off me. I thought I would return to school, to my friends, and to the life that I treasured.

Unfortunately, I was wrong.

As soon as I returned home with a modified cast that permitted me to sit upright, I began feeling very sick. I frequently felt nauseous and found it difficult to take a deep breath. One night, I awakened feeling violently ill and was taken by ambulance to the hospital, where I was diagnosed with pneumonia.

The next day I was rushed back to Cleveland and placed in ICU. At thirteen years old, I did not know what those letters meant, but I soon realized that if you are placed in the ICU, you are very sick and you never get any rest. My left lung had collapsed, and I was placed inside an oxygen tent. My lungs were suctioned hourly through a rubber tube in my nose. I was in critical condition, and my life hung in the balance. I spent sixteen days in this inhospitable environment, and I remember feeling so harassed and afraid. Even though the lights were never turned off in my room, it was one of the darkest periods of my life.

Although I had to spend the better part of each day inside the cold, humid atmosphere of the oxygen tent, my mother spent hour after hour exhorting me to not give up.

I vividly remember her daily sermon that began, "God has not brought you this far to fail. He has a special mission for you to perform. You are going to get better. You will recover from this illness. You will forget about the times that we spent together here. You will achieve great things. You will forget how bad things have been."

I would reply, "Mom, I won't forget." Then I would say, "I just want to get better and go home."

One day, Mom couldn't rouse me from my environment of discouragement. I was tired of being sick. I felt like giving up. I felt like surrendering.

I told her, "Mom, I am tired of all of the prayers and all of the sermons and all of the pep talks. I am not getting better!"

She had taught me that there is purpose in trial, and she had an answer for me. She had purchased a small Bible containing both the Old and New Testaments. It was lightweight enough for me to hold while prone on my back. She said, "Here, if you are tired of listening to me, then maybe you can find something to read that will help you."

I grudgingly accepted her invitation and took the Bible from her hands. I opened it and eventually found Psalm 86:

Bow down thine ear, O Lord, hear me: for I am poor and needy.

Preserve my soul; for I am holy: O thou my God, save thy servant that trusteth in thee.

Be merciful unto me, O Lord: for I cry unto thee daily.

Rejoice the soul of thy servant: for unto thee, O Lord, do I lift up my soul.

For thou, Lord, art good, and ready to forgive; and plenteous in mercy unto all them that call upon thee.

Give ear, O Lord, unto my prayer; and attend to the voice of my supplications.

In the day of my trouble I will call upon thee: for thou wilt answer me.

Among the gods there is none like unto thee, O Lord; neither are there any works like unto thy works.

All nations whom thou hast made shall come and worship before thee, O Lord; and shall glorify thy name.

For thou art great, and doest wondrous things: thou art God alone.

Teach me thy way, O Lord; I will walk in thy truth: unite my heart to fear thy name.

I will praise thee, O Lord my God, with all my heart: and I will glorify thy name for evermore.

For great is thy mercy toward me: and thou hast delivered my soul from the lowest hell.

O God, the proud are risen against me, and the assemblies of violent men have sought after my soul; and have not set thee before them.

But thou, O Lord, art a God full of compassion, and gracious, longsuffering, and plenteous in mercy and truth.

O turn unto me, and have mercy upon me; give thy strength unto thy servant, and save the son of thine handmaid.

Shew me a token for good; that they which hate me may see it, and be ashamed: because thou, Lord, hast holpen me, and comforted me.

I was only thirteen years old, but I had never read anything that pierced my soul with as much power as this particular passage.

It was entitled "A Prayer of David," but I felt as if I had uttered the words. I felt as if King David had captured my feelings of desperation and isolation. I felt as though someone understood what I was experiencing and how low my emotions were. David may have said the prayer, but it was mine as well.

Suddenly, I did not feel so alone. David had experienced what I had experienced. That moment and the discovery of that prayer stand as one of the most powerfully spiritual events of my life.

I, as David, was poor and needy. I was asking the Lord to turn His attention and compassion toward me. I needed Him. I needed to be reassured again that He was close by and aware of my suffering and agony. I had lost hope. I had lost faith. I had lost my way.

Psalm 86 rescued my soul.

I asked that the Lord be merciful. I knew even then that if my mother and I had joined in daily, fervent prayer, mighty prayer, that somehow we would get through this latest ordeal. But, I knew then as I know now, that we cannot overcome the things that terrorize and overwhelm us by ourselves. We need help. We need divine help. We need God's help.

Prayers can be many things: questions, hymns, reports, requests, discussions, monologues, declarations, proclamations, or testimonies.

But during tough times, really tough times, prayers are what David says they are: cries for help.

And I was crying for help.

I remember sitting inside that oxygen tank, with cold air blowing on my face, thinking, at last, someone knew how I felt. David did!

I found hope and confidence in David's prayer. It is the type of hope and confidence that we all need and seek for during trials and times when our faith is being tested.

David knew what I needed to know. He confirmed what I had since forgotten. I had not been forsaken. Not only could I still pray, but David assured me that I was entitled, as a son of God, to an answer! Notice the confidence contained in this verse: "In the day of my trouble I will call upon thee: for thou wilt answer me" (Psalm 86:7).

David knew no matter how bad it got, God would answer his prayer. I also knew that I would get an answer.

David knew that relief in his suffering would come, because he realized and remembered who God was and is. He is the same yesterday, today, and tomorrow, no matter what we are asked to endure.

David acknowledges God for who He is! He is all-powerful and all-knowing. He is truly God. He is absolutely the Almighty God! As I read the words from David's prayer, they reminded me of what I had forgotten. I needed to remember God no matter what I was going through.

I turned my attention to these powerful, descriptive words about our Lord:

> Among the gods there is none like unto thee, O Lord; neither are there any works like unto thy works.
>
> All nations whom thou hast made shall come and worship before thee, O Lord; and shall glorify thy name.
>
> For thou art great, and doest wondrous things: thou art God alone.
>
> Teach me thy way, O Lord; I will walk in thy truth: unite my heart to fear thy name.
>
> I will praise thee, O Lord my God, with all my heart: and I will glorify thy name for evermore. (Psalm 86:8–12)

I had reached that point of humility that many of us reach when going through heart-wrenching trials and moments of agony. I recognized how low I was and how much I needed God's help.

I, like David, recognized that God is all-powerful. Nothing can defeat Him. Nothing surprises Him. Nothing discourages Him. And nothing is beyond His capacity to overcome.

Although I was lying in a hospital bed, I remember feeling that

I was flinging my body at Heavenly Father's feet. I was crying out before my Maker: "Help me."

I was basically saying, "Heavenly Father, I submit my will and my life into your hands. I simply cannot take this agony any longer. Please make it stop. I am tired of all of the pain and the probing by those individuals treating me. Please help me feel better. Please let me go home."

I knew that He knew how I felt. Psalm 86 had reconfirmed the truth that I had learned only six months earlier when my spine was fused: God does hear and answer prayers. He knew who I was in July 1968, and He knew what I was being subjected to in January 1969. Heavenly Father does not take vacations. He is always available. He is always accessible. He is always aware of what you and I are subjected to as part of our earthly experiences. He knows. He cares. And He helps.

He is exactly who David says He is. There is no God like Him. There is no God before Him.

There is no challenge, no affliction, that is beyond His touch. There is nothing in this world or in any other world that makes Him flinch or causes Him to turn away.

In times of stress, it is important to understand the critical relationship between Heavenly Father and us. We are God's children. At some point or points in our lives, we are asked to pass through terrifying and frightening things. But those things do not change Him. They do not change His character or His nature. They do not change His involvement or His awareness. They do not change His power. Most important, they do not change His abiding love for us—for you and me. He does not cease to be God because of what you and I are asked to go through as part of mortality.

As David correctly recognized during his agony, we must realize that God is still God. His nature and power and knowledge do not change. It is His plan, not ours. It is His world, not ours.

David's prayer also demonstrated to me what I needed to do or could do during a very stressful period of my life. In verses 11 and 12, David asks the Lord to teach him and expresses his desire to walk in His truth. David then says he wants to unite his heart to fear God's name. Consequently, David recognizes that he cannot be passive during this difficult challenge. David taught me that I had things to do. I needed to remain hopeful, prayerful, faithful, and obedient to God's commandments and His teachings.

Most important, for David and for all of us, David swore his allegiance to God. He promised God that he would not abandon Him. He states unequivocally, "I will praise thee, O Lord my God, with all my heart: and I will glorify thy name for evermore" (Psalm 86:12).

I have always believed since reading those words that praising God is a very critical component in our daily devotionals. To praise God is more than singing a hymn, although that is a very worshipful manifestation of our love and reverence for Him. Praising God is understanding and remembering and testifying who He is and what He has done to confirm who He is throughout our lives.

That is what I believe my mother tried to teach me as she counseled me while I suffered during those sixteen horrifying days in the intensive care unit. She told me that I would forget. I told her I would not.

I have not forgotten those sixteen days. I have not forgotten Him. I have not forgotten David's prayer. I have not forgotten how God comforted me in my fear, my longing, and my suffering. And I have not forgotten to praise His glorious name forevermore.

CHAPTER FIVE

"THE TENDER MERCIES OF THE LORD"

After witnessing a child's suffering and anguish and having to endure one hospitalization after another, there is a natural inclination for parents to protect the child from further trauma. It was painful for my parents to see me subjected to trial after trial. It would have been totally understandable if they had simply kept me close to them for the remainder of their lives or my life.

I had defied every doctor's prediction of a premature death. I had certainly come close to death on a number of occasions, but I had come to know that the purpose of my life was not to merely survive hospitalizations or to simply beat the odds of prognosis after prognosis that I would live an abbreviated life.

Ever since I had seen the photographs of FDR when I was four years old, I desired to succeed and to achieve. Because of that magazine and my parents' faith in me, I was driven by the image and legacy of my hero—the president of the United States in a wheelchair.

Mom also instilled in me a belief that I had come to her and to

My family enjoying the Easter parade, New York, 1959.

this earth for a reason—there were significant things for me to accomplish. There were so many things to look forward to. In spite of my disabilities, I did not simply want to survive; I wanted to thrive.

This passion to live a significant life required me to stand on my own two feet—figuratively speaking. I had to learn how to achieve goals and overcome adversity in all areas of my life. My parents could not protect me forever from the world or the wilderness.

Nor did they want to. My father often said, "We are not going to live forever. You need to get as much schooling as you can and learn to live on your own. Mom and Dad are not going to be here forever." I remember my father also saying that one of the greatest gifts that a parent can give to a child is a great education. My father was determined that all his children would receive that treasure—including me.

Although he did not hold the priesthood until 1983, when he

joined the Church, Dad always had a sound understanding of the purposes of life. He understood that we all must be tested in mortality. It was his view that we are all given talents and gifts that need to be developed and shared and that we all have dreams and aspirations no matter our disabilities or weaknesses. He firmly believed that we all deserved an education. More, he felt we had the obligation to acquire knowledge so that we could grow and help others grow.

Needless to say, getting an education was critically important in my family. Mother would often say, "Unto whom much is given much is required" (D&C 82:3). I was not excused from expectations simply because I was disabled.

We all agreed I needed an education so that I could experience life and enjoy it to its fullest. I needed to exercise the gift of agency. I had choices to make. I had opportunities to explore. I had talents to discover, to refine, and to strengthen. I had both the will to live and the desire to achieve. It did not matter that I had been denied the ability to stand, walk, and run. I had a brain that needed to be utilized. It was time for me to learn as much as I could and to prepare for life outside the comfort and shelter of my parents' loving arms.

When it was time for me to enter kindergarten, every elementary school had stairs. However, I was still lightweight enough that my mother or my father could carry me into the building. The first educational obstacle to be overcome was not architecture but attitude.

The simple fact was no principal or teacher was willing to give me the chance to be educated, except one—a diminutive teacher named Mrs. Walton. She was no more than four feet, eight inches tall, but she stood as a towering beam of light to my educational pursuits and introduction into living life with a disability.

Mrs. Walton had been Carole's kindergarten teacher, and she was delighted to accept the responsibility and the privilege of being my first teacher. There was one problem: the school where Mrs. Walton taught was outside my school district boundaries, and the school board rejected her request for an exception. I would not be allowed to attend kindergarten with Mrs. Walton.

Mrs. Walton was distraught. Mom was discouraged. Dad was outraged.

He instantly asked for the item to be placed on the agenda at the next school board meeting. At that meeting, my father declared, "My son deserves an education just like any other child in this town. Just because he is in a wheelchair does not mean that he cannot learn. If you deny his chance to be educated, I will sue you."

There was a second vote, and the school board reversed its decision. It was not a unanimous vote; it did not have to be.

I just needed the chance, and my father made certain I was given that chance!

<hr />

By the time I reached middle school, my older siblings, Carole and Billy, had left home to attend prep schools in Pennsylvania. However, those schools required each student to live on campus. Such an option was unavailable to me since my care required parental supervision.

Still, that did not discourage my father from exploring the possibility that I, too, could be educated in a highly competitive academic environment. In his initial search he found there were no known day-schools in Ohio or Pennsylvania where the students were allowed to live at home rather than live in dormitories.

My father did not give up. In a second search, he found the perfect fit. It was Sewickley Academy in Sewickley, Pennsylvania, a suburb of Pittsburgh and located only forty miles from our home in Ohio. The Senior School, where I would attend, was fortuitously built on one floor. There were no stairs!

The headmaster of the school was a visionary man named James Cavalier, who welcomed the opportunity for the academy to have its first full-time wheelchair student. Nothing was an obstacle for "Mr. Cav," as the students called him. He was a great facilitator and problem-solver. In his way of thinking, there was no obstacle that did not have a solution.

My parents did not know where I could live, but Mr. Cav had already thought of that. He knew of an apartment building a block away from the school where my mother, younger sister Judy, and I could live during the week.

We did not know who would help Mother bathe and dress me in the mornings and put me to bed at night. Again, Mr. Cav had the answer. There was a special facility for young people with disabilities located just up the street. Soon, my parents had hired two ideal nurses.

I remember the glee on my parents' faces as they shared the news that they had found the right school for me. This adventure would take courage on all of our parts. It would take a great sacrifice for my parents because they would be together only on weekends. It would take creativity and imagination and faith to meet the unforeseen challenges and choices that lay ahead, but as Mom always said, "The Lord will provide; He always does." The gift of education was worth it. The attainment of knowledge would further bless my life and enable me to realize my gifts and share them.

This experience, once again, underscored an important lesson in my life—and in all of our lives. My mother referred to this principle as "it only takes one."

Whenever I would express fear that I was going to be denied an opportunity, Mom would simply say, "Remember, it only takes one."

After all, it only took one magazine to help me accept my disability and believe that my life could touch others.

It only took one headmaster at a country day-school to welcome me.

Nephi said, "I . . . will show unto you that the tender mercies of the Lord are over all those whom he hath chosen, because of their faith, to make them mighty even unto the power of deliverance" (1 Nephi 1:20).

I was learning that if we have the desire, the hope, the faith, and the patience, the Lord provides the tender mercy.

It is interesting to note that after the Saints were driven from Missouri to Illinois, they found a place on the Mississippi River and named it Nauvoo. They were poor. They were persecuted. They were barely surviving. And yet, their desire to learn and to be educated had not been reduced by the angry mobs that harassed and stalked them. In 1840, Joseph Smith included within his petition to incorporate the city of Nauvoo, Illinois, "An institution of learning within the limits of the city, for the teaching of the Arts, Sciences, and Learned Professions, to be called the 'University of the City of Nauvoo'" (Smith, *History of the Church*, 4:243).

In fact, the charter of this university in Nauvoo served as the foundation for the University of Deseret, which later became known as the University of Utah, which was established by Brigham Young in 1850.

Brigham Young once explained, "Education is the power to think clearly, the power to act well in the world's work, and the power to appreciate life" (Young, in "The Brigham Young University," 831).

Reinforcing the importance of education, President Henry B. Eyring (then a member of the Quorum of the Twelve Apostles) observed, "When the Saints in Utah were still struggling to produce enough food to live, they started schools. They felt driven to lift their children toward light and to greater usefulness by education. That drive is more than a cultural tradition passed on through the generations. It is the natural fruit of living the gospel of Jesus Christ" (Eyring, "Education for Real Life," 15).

My parents taught me that I was no different than anyone else. Believing that to be true, I often told my mother during my childhood, "I am just like everyone else, I just sit all of the time." Education was the road that would lead me to my dream of being accepted. Education was the means whereby I could obtain greater knowledge of the world and of my mission in the world. Certainly, my muscles could not grow, but my intellect and knowledge and understanding of how the world worked could progress and increase.

With education comes information and choices and preparation, all of which provide an increased awareness of who we are and what we can become. Education draws us closer to the truth of all things. It also makes us useful to other people rather than a burden to them. In spite of my physical disability, I knew I had something to contribute and that education would be the means of delivering it. Though I wasn't acquainted with him yet, I believed what the Prophet Joseph said when he declared, "Knowledge is power" (Smith, *History of the Church*, 5:392).

The Prophet Joseph Smith explained both the sum and substance of learning when he recorded:

> Teach ye diligently and my grace shall attend you, that you may be instructed more perfectly in theory, in principle, in doctrine, in the law of the gospel, in all things that pertain unto the kingdom of God, that are expedient for you to understand;
>
> Of things both in heaven and in the earth, and under the earth; things which have been, things which are, things which must shortly come to pass; things which are at home, things which are abroad; the wars and the perplexities of the nations, and the judgments which are on the land; and a knowledge also of countries and of kingdoms—
>
> That ye may be prepared in all things when I shall send you again to magnify the calling whereunto I have called you, and the mission with which I have commissioned you. (D&C 88:78–80)

Part of my incentive to gain an education was my desire for increased participation and integration into the lives of my classmates. The fact that I lived my life in a wheelchair did not preclude me from the desire to be liked by others. I did not want to spend my life being isolated or separated. In short, I wanted to feel as though I belonged to a class, a school, and a body of students.

My mother would tell me that it was my responsibility to make children comfortable about who I was. She explained that children would be reluctant to interact with me because of certain fears and myths that they held toward people in wheelchairs. It was my responsibility to initiate the process of acceptance. I was different, and I knew that others were hesitant to engage me, to approach me, and to include me. Mom said, "To be liked, you need to be likeable."

I soon learned that my sense of humor and ability to laugh overcame many stereotypes about my disability. My mother pointed out that my smile and laugh would attract friends and reassure them that I was not sad about being disabled. She would say, "No one likes to be around someone who is unhappy." Putting on a happy face did not take effort. I was happy being me, and I wanted children to like me.

Children often said that I sounded like a seal when I laughed. It was distinct. It was unique. My happiness drew children to me. My laughter made everyone in the room happier, including my teachers.

In addition to my contagious laugh, there was another aspect of my boyhood that helped me to become likeable and draw others to me: my love of sports.

My brother, Billy, and I loved every sport, but especially basketball, football, and baseball. We knew the players, the teams, and the statistics.

Not only did we read every sports magazine, but we played all of the sports. Billy had the gift of improvisation and he adapted every sport, modifying the rules in such a way that we could compete on an equal footing, even with my disability. For instance, a traditional baseball bat and ball were too heavy for me to hold, so we played Whiffle ball instead, which utilized a plastic bat and ball.

Every summer night Billy and I would play on our driveway. Billy would assume the batting stances of our boyhood heroes: Hank Aaron, Roberto Clemente, and Willie Mays. He would announce every game and even supply the cheers of the crowd. It was a magical, pretend world that was free from discrimination and rejection.

I was able to pitch to him by lifting my right arm with my left arm and then throwing my body forward to propel the ball toward home plate. Billy never tired from chasing his batted balls that landed across the street in our neighbor's yard.

We never cared who won or who lost. That is not why we played. We were together. We were brothers. We were the original "boys of summer," and even now, when I feel the humidity and see the dwindling light of day on a summer evening, I go back to those priceless times with Billy. They still stand as some of the sweetest memories of my life.

I played hard, but I studied even harder. I never took my intellectual gift for granted. Mother would remind me that it came from God and I needed to bless the lives of others with it.

I loved competing in the classroom. That is what my father challenged me to do when he showed me that magazine when I was four years old. He always said that grades were important. I paid attention. I took him at his word.

My junior class in prep school had only sixty-eight students. Each was competitive and ambitious in seeking admission into the best colleges in America. Though I was disabled physically, I wanted the same thing.

Mr. Cav suggested that I limit myself to applying only to wheelchair-friendly schools. There were a few, at that time, including the University of Illinois and a small Presbyterian college in North Carolina. But, as I explained to my mother and to Mr. Cavalier, if I were to go to such a college, it would simply delay my entrance into the real world where both architectural and attitudinal barriers existed for people with disabilities.

Ready for my high school prom.

I made good grades. I wrote for the school newspaper. I sang in the choir. I was as able as any other applicant.

I added one more achievement to my high school resume that made me unique. In the fall of my senior year, Mr. Cav gathered us in a classroom to hold elections. As each office was announced, the most popular students were nominated. He asked for nominations for class president, and three students who had attended the academy for years were named as candidates. Then a friend of mine placed my name into nomination. My immediate thought was that I had no chance. I had only attended the academy for one year; I had not been there long enough. I was not as well-known or as popular or as likeable as my classmates. Or so I thought.

Mr. Cav asked all of us who had been nominated to close our eyes and place our heads on our desks as he counted the votes. When I opened my eyes, everyone was staring at me and then they began cheering and applauding. I had been elected!

I could not contain my tears of joy! It only takes one!

CHAPTER SIX

———◦⊶⬥⊷◦———

"IF ANY OF YOU
LACK WISDOM, LET
HIM ASK OF GOD"

Change is a fundamental and essential part of our lives. With change comes a variety of challenges and choices, and with them, opportunities and possibilities for growth and increased faith. Changes come to us at every age and crossroad of life. Change is difficult. Often it is hard and vexing. Sometimes it is exciting and rejuvenating.

Given our innate independence and inclination to resist conforming, change is necessary for discipleship. As Elder Marvin J. Ashton once said, "We need not feel that we must forever be what we presently are. There is a tendency to think of change as the enemy. Many of us are suspect of change and will often fight and resist it before we have even discovered what the actual effects will be. When change is thought through carefully, it can produce the most rewarding and profound experiences in life. The changes we make must fit the Lord's purpose and patterns" ("Progress through Change," 61). Change is indeed part of Heavenly Father's plan of happiness. Change provides us with the opportunity to learn more about our Lord and to trust His love and promises for each of us.

We also experience change in our relationships, our employment, and even in our health and our bodies. We face changing economic circumstances. It appears as if everything is subject to change.

But we are not left alone; we are not abandoned. Our loving Godhead is there to comfort and guide us through these changing times.

One of the great changes that I faced was one that many of us experience: I wanted to leave home and go to college.

It was never a question of *if* I would go to college. That much was in my control. My grades and standardized test scores were competitive enough to allow me to apply to and ultimately be accepted by three very good colleges, namely: Duke, Vanderbilt, and Emory.

The biggest question on my horizon was how I would even survive at college. How would I deal with all of the changes that would take place and the demands that would be asked of me in order to begin a new life as a college student?

Just like most freshman, I worried about whether I could compete. I wondered about choosing my major. I was curious whether I might meet someone whom I might fall in love with.

But unlike most freshmen, I had an additional array of seemingly endless questions about my physical safety and care that caused me much anxiety. Who would shower and dress me? Where would I live? How would I get to class? Who would help me with meals? Who would help me go to the bathroom? Who would put me to bed and turn me over at night? Would my parents have to employ professional staff as they did at prep school, or would my mother have to escort me to and from every class? The idea of relying on my mother did not feel much like a college experience. As much as I loved her, I never desired to go to college with my mother as my chaperone.

Clearly, I would not be a typical freshman. I could not care for myself, and I would have to navigate campus in a motorized wheelchair. I would be a unique student trying to find his way on a new frontier. It was a daunting and somewhat frightening undertaking. I knew there would be many challenges and changes ahead, but that did not discourage me from hoping and believing that somehow, some way, my dream of attending college would materialize. Mother always said, "God will lead us to the right place, if it is His will." I believed her.

<hr/>

My mother's conversion to The Church of Jesus Christ of Latter-day Saints helped form the foundation of my own growing faith. Her story corroborates that God often "moves in a mysterious way His wonders to perform" (*Hymns,* no. 285). Although my mother was raised in the Serbian Orthodox Church, she began attending various churches with different roommates and friends while she was attending West Virginia University. There she enrolled in a humanities course that traced the development of the Catholic and Protestant churches, and she studied such reformers as Martin Luther, John Wesley, and John Calvin. Her study of religion spurred questions. She later wrote, "I began to wonder, why, if there was only one God, we do not all worship him the same way? Why were men led by the interpretations of the scriptures by other men? Why did not Jesus Christ, when He was on the earth, tell men how to worship Him?"

Upon her graduation, Mother returned to her hometown of Weirton, West Virginia, began teaching high school chemistry, and resumed attending the Serbian Church. Then she married and felt as though her religious education had reached a plateau.

When I was admitted as a toddler to the National Institutes of Health for examination, Mother was devastated. But it was there that she met an elderly woman whose husband was a cancer patient at NIH. The woman gave her a book that taught Mom a new way of praying. The book encouraged readers to talk to God directly and about specific issues, rather than reciting rote prayers. Mother later wrote, "One night, as I was on my knees pouring out my heart to my Heavenly Father, asking the Lord to preserve Stevie's life, I felt a presence in my room. I was alone in a strange place and strange city (Washington, D.C.), pregnant [with her fourth child], and tired. I became frightened and I turned up the lights. But I never forgot that feeling."

The days following the diagnosis of my disease was a dark time for her. She recalled, "As we took our baby home, I fought bouts of depression constantly, until finally my husband jolted my whole being one day by stating, 'You don't have any faith.'"

Mother was incensed. She recalled, "Who was it who prayed continuously day and night? [But] I soon realized my demeanor belied my faith. If I was to pray, I was going to have to believe that I would receive [an answer]."

At this time, Mother began memorizing certain scriptures. Her favorite was from the book of John, "Peace I leave with you, my peace I give unto you: not as the world giveth, give I unto you. Let not your heart be troubled, neither let it be afraid" (John 14:27). She often said that that particular scripture calmed her and gave her strength.

Then came her meeting with the two missionaries in 1959, and from that point on, every time she saw them walking in our town, she would explain to whoever was with her, "Those are Mormon missionaries."

With the birth of her fourth child, a healthy daughter she named Judith Hope, Mother noted, "We had outgrown our home. Our little house was getting crowded. So, two years later we moved into a large house in a different neighborhood. Stevie was in his fifth year. Although he wasn't able to walk, he turned from a frail, sickly child, to an outgoing, very talkative, and bright little boy. We particularly enjoyed his language skills, and although we quaked at every sneeze, we learned to relax and enjoy him and take one day at a time."

One day, our housekeeper, Helen, told Mom that there were two missionaries at the door. When she asked whether she should turn them away, Mother replied, "No, I want to speak to them." The missionaries introduced themselves, and to their astonishment, Mother replied, "Oh, yes, you are Mormons!" She told them that she would like to know more, and they gave her a pamphlet describing the First Vision. After reading it, she knew it was true. She, like Joseph Smith, had wondered why there were so many churches. She remembered the presence she had felt in her room at the National Institutes of Health in Washington, D.C., when she had prayed and asked God to let her keep her baby.

With her typical candor, she explained, "The Joseph Smith story was not hard for me to accept. I [immediately] believed it." She also recalled, "Then came a moment of truth. I had to tell my husband that I was studying Mormonism and that I wanted to be baptized! His initial shock turned to hurt because I had taken the lessons without his knowledge."

When the missionaries asked my father for his permission

that Mother be baptized, he simply said, "That is her decision, not mine."

Mother later reflected, "He allowed me something that I had only recently learned—that I had my agency. He loved and respected me enough to trust my judgment."

Following her baptism, in the blessing given her as she was confirmed, Mother was promised that she would bring her family into the Church. She was skeptical. She did not believe she had the influence or power to convert her family. Initially, her choice to be baptized was focused exclusively upon her own needs and desires. She later explained, "At that time, I remember wanting this just for me—I needed it, I desired it. It had not entered my mind that my family would embark on this venture of undertaking a new religion. It was enough for me to handle my own thoughts and accompanying problems."

The missionaries counseled Mother not to make the gospel a bone of contention in her home. When she asked how she could approach my father to begin making financial donations to the Church, the missionaries responded, "Sister Mikita, the Church doesn't need your money." They told her that her example was a sufficient sacrifice.

Following this advice, she remembers, "I tried to be wise. I did not try to force my children into accepting the gospel. We had prayer at every meal and together in the evenings. We read Bible stories, we discussed the Episcopal sermon at lunch each Sunday. We listened to find what we agreed with and what we did not [agree with in those sermons]."

Although in the early years following her conversion Mother did not attend the small branch regularly, each ensuing pair of missionaries would visit her. Mother explained her interactions with the missionaries and her subtle teaching strategies with her children in

*My family gathered in Steubenville, Ohio, to celebrate Judith's
wedding day, August 17, 1980.*

these words: "They had lunch with us, gave blessings to my sick
children, and taught us more about the gospel. My children shed
many tears as each pair would leave to be replaced by others that we
learned to love." Even though my father did not have the priesthood,
Mother was counseled to respect him as though he did. When, at
one particular point, Mother desired that all of us should be baptized, my father issued a conditional denial. He explained that we
were too young to make such a decision for ourselves. But, in time,
if we elected to convert as informed individuals, then he would support those decisions. Once again, Dad not only understood but also
respected the principle of agency.

<hr />

Although I was not yet a Latter-day Saint, I still had faith in the
words of my mother and believed that God had a plan for my life.
Consequently, I had what could be termed as an "active faith." I was
actively and anxiously seeking out and doing my part in obtaining
guidance and inspiration.

My parents and I discussed in detail my dream to attend college. We had talked about it since I was a boy. I had applied myself in my studies. I considered many colleges. Then, I was accepted.

But being accepted to these fine institutions was not enough. Our search and efforts continued. We needed more information. We needed to visit each college and gather more data before we could make our decision and then ask the Lord for His blessing.

Faith is an active thing. Faith requires confidence and effort. Faith requires courage, research, and sacrifice. Faith demands that you and I act.

The young Joseph Smith was one of the greatest examples of a simple, yet active, faith. He recites the formula for dealing with change in our lives:

> My mind at times was greatly excited, the cry and tumult were so great and incessant. The Presbyterians were most decided against the Baptists and Methodists, and used all the powers of both reason and sophistry to prove their errors, or, at least, to make the people think they were in error. On the other hand, the Baptists and Methodists in their turn were equally zealous in endeavoring to establish their own tenets and disprove all others.
>
> In the midst of this war of words and tumult of opinions, I often said to myself: What is to be done? Who of all these parties are right; or, are they all wrong together? If any one of them be right, which is it, and how shall I know it? (Joseph Smith–History 1:9–10)

Joseph thought about the subject of religion. He considered the different denominations. He pondered what was being said and the implications of what was being taught. Though he may not have initially perceived it in exactly these terms, he was vigorously engaged in searching out truth and clarity for his life and for his future.

Joseph did more than think and ponder about the religious fervor that surrounded him. As he explains:

> During this time of great excitement my mind was called up to serious reflection and great uneasiness; but though my feelings were deep and often poignant, still I kept myself aloof from all these parties, though I attended their several meetings as often as occasion would permit. In process of time my mind became somewhat partial to the Methodist sect, and I felt some desire to be united with them; but so great were the confusion and strife among the different denominations, that it was impossible for a person young as I was, and so unacquainted with men and things, to come to any certain conclusion who was right and who was wrong. (Joseph Smith–History 1:8)

Joseph's desire for an answer did not cloud his judgment or accelerate the pace of his decision. He did not rush his process. He needed more time and information. He attended some meetings, but those were inadequate to persuade him.

His faith and desire drove him to more effort and actions. Indeed, this was a stressful time in his life. Yet Joseph did not relent. He allowed his faith to propel him into the scriptures and then into a now-sacred grove of trees.

> While I was laboring under the extreme difficulties caused by the contests of these parties of religionists, I was one day reading the Epistle of James, first chapter and fifth verse, which reads: If any of you lack wisdom, let him ask

of God, that giveth to all men liberally, and upbraideth not; and it shall be given him.

Never did any passage of scripture come with more power to the heart of man than this did at this time to mine. It seemed to enter with great force into every feeling of my heart. I reflected on it again and again, knowing that if any person needed wisdom from God, I did; for how to act I did not know, and unless I could get more wisdom than I then had, I would never know; for the teachers of religion of the different sects understood the same passages of scripture so differently as to destroy all confidence in set- tling the question by an appeal to the Bible.

At length I came to the conclusion that I must either re- main in darkness and confusion, or else I must do as James directs, that is, ask of God. I at length came to the determi- nation to "ask of God," concluding that if he gave wisdom to them that lacked wisdom, and would give liberally, and not upbraid, I might venture.

So, in accordance with this, my determination to ask of God, I retired to the woods to make the attempt. It was on the morning of a beautiful, clear day, early in the spring of eighteen hundred and twenty. It was the first time in my life that I had made such an attempt, for amidst all my anxieties I had never as yet made the attempt to pray vocally. (Joseph Smith–History 1:11–14)

Joseph knew the location where he would offer his first vocal prayer. He had considered the place. He took himself as far as his young faith could take him. He had done the work, and he was pre- pared to ask and receive his divine answer.

> After I had retired to the place where I had previously
> designed to go, having looked around me, and finding
> myself alone, I kneeled down and began to offer up the
> desires of my heart to God. (Joseph Smith–History 1:15)

After all, "Faith without works is dead" (James 2:20).

⎯⎯⎯⎯◦⎯⎯⎯⎯

When it came to deciding which college was the right choice for
me, we faced uncertainty, doubt, and indecision. We were open to
inspiration, and we were prepared to act on the basis of that inspiration, but we needed more information and more faith.

I succeeded in persuading Mr. Cavalier and my parents that I
did not want to attend a wheelchair-friendly college. I appealed to
their logic by pointing out that since I would have to survive for the
rest of my life in a challenging wilderness of curbs, stereotypes, and
other barriers associated with people with disabilities, I needed to
begin experiencing life in the real world at a real college. It would be
difficult, but that was part of living life in a wheelchair.

I always feared that my father's vision of my attending college
alongside my mother and close to our home in Ohio would prevail.
I resisted that at all levels. I wanted to prove to myself that I could
not only survive but also thrive on my own. I needed the chance and
the opportunity.

I was definitely proclaiming myself as a student pioneer. There
were not many individuals with my degree of disability in America
in the 1970s who had attended college. I knew I was facing significant obstacles.

In the spring of 1974, after visiting Vanderbilt University in
Nashville and Emory University in Atlanta, we were very discouraged.

We were met with chilly receptions, and officials at both schools appeared apathetic to our basic questions of where I could live and who might be able to help in caring for me. They offered inadequate answers and no satisfactory solutions. To put it bluntly, I was not welcome at either school.

That left only Duke University, which remained my last hope to attend college as independently as possible. For me, attending college independent of my parents represented more than a traditional rite of passage; it represented entrance into the world where I would live the rest of my life. It was a symbol of personal freedom and responsible adulthood.

While driving from the airport to the Duke campus, my father criticized me for failing to apply to the University of Pittsburgh or Ohio State University so that I could be closer to home, which would allow my mother to stay with me.

I was so afraid that my father was correct. He almost convinced me that I had misjudged my capacity to achieve my goal. I doubted my intentions and felt defeated. I could not hold back the tears as we drove onto the Duke campus. I could not bear receiving more bad news.

But then the faith of my mother once again intervened. We were not out of options. We were not without hope. We were not alone. Mother insisted that we pray before our meeting with the dean of student affairs, James Douthat. Mother asked God to bless us with guidance and inspiration. She pleaded that the hearts of those individuals with whom we would be meeting would be softened and that they would be receptive to me. She asked God for His will to be revealed. It was not the first time that I had heard this prayer. My mother was praying for a miracle! Then we acted on her prayer and her faith. We got out of the car and entered the administration building. We were prepared to receive our answer.

Her prayer was as prophetic as it was reassuring. As soon as we met Dean Douthat, we knew that Mother's prayer was being answered. My dream was going to be realized! Another door had been opened! My choice was clear. There was much light in that office.

What we found inside his office was more than a dean of students. We found a visionary and friend. Jim Douthat was a consummate Southern gentleman. He had a calm, yet confident, aura.

He commenced by laying out his plan for my life for the next four years. He said, "Stephen, you're the first wheelchair freshman in the history of this university. We are delighted to have you, and we will do everything within our power to make this experience as meaningful and enjoyable as possible. Welcome to Duke."

There was only one dormitory on campus that featured an elevator, so that was where I would live. If curbs required beveling, then the university would bevel them. I would be assigned a permanent, reserved parking space outside my dormitory. If I selected classes in inaccessible buildings, then Dean Douthat would ensure that the class was moved into a building that had an elevator. He would hand-carry my class schedule every semester over the next four years. It is hard to imagine these extraordinary accommodations and modifications being made at that point in America's history. It would still be twenty years until the Americans with Disabilities Act of 1990 would become federal law—which requires public places to be more user-friendly to millions of Americans with disabilities.

It was as if Dean Douthat had passed a personal act of Congress specifically to allow me to fulfill my dream of attending college on my terms. It was that revelatory and that miraculous. Duke wanted me as much as I needed Duke.

Within five minutes of meeting Dean Douthat, I had found my university. I had found a home. I had found a guardian angel. But my angel was clothed in a seersucker suit and spoke with a Southern

With Dean Douthat and his wife, 1978.

drawl! It was as if he had been prepared years before to smooth a pathway which previously had appeared so formidable and rocky.

My parents and I left Dean Douthat's office with tears streaming down our cheeks. Before leaving the campus, Mother insisted that we go to the towering Duke Chapel at the center of the university complex. It was a weekday so there was no one else in the chapel that afternoon—just the three of us giving thanks for the miracle we had experienced.

I knew we had been guided to Duke University. For me, it was a land full of promise and hope. We knew we had been blessed to meet such a gracious, kind, receptive, and good man as Dean Douthat.

Once again, Mom was right. So long as we had active faith, it only took one—one extraordinary university and one understanding heart—to open the way. "The effectual fervent prayer of a righteous man [or woman] availeth much" (James 5:16). We should give thanks for the effectual, fervent prayers offered on our behalf by the righteous men and women in our lives.

Elder David A. Bednar explained, "We press forward and persevere in the consecrated work of prayer, after we say 'amen,' by acting upon the things we have expressed to Heavenly Father. Asking in faith requires honesty, effort, commitment, and persistence" (Bednar, "Ask in Faith," 95).

Pressing forward at Duke University would take much honesty, effort, commitment, and persistence on my part. But it would also take something even more powerful and extraordinary: the goodwill and generosity of my fellow students.

Initially, we believed that I would be able to rely almost entirely on the help of a single roommate to dress me for classes in the mornings and to stay with me during the night. That plan was a colossal failure from the start.

My roommate was not a good fit. In fact, he was smaller than I was and weighed less than I did!

After meeting him, I remarked to my mother, "Am I supposed to lift him into bed, or the other way around?" We both laughed, but that comic moment did not last long.

He showed very little interest in helping me, and his indifference jeopardized my future at Duke. In addition to his lack of support, I became sick during my first semester. The doctors diagnosed the flu. But their prescription for a cure also included advising me to go home and not return to Duke. They said the rigors of the Duke experience were not tailored for someone as medically fragile as I. Not surprisingly, my father agreed that I should come home. But Dad was back in Ohio, and Mother was still in North Carolina with me.

I begged my mother to let me stay. She said that if we could create a better system of helpers, she could convince my father that I could stay. That was the problem; we had no idea what that system would look like.

We approached Dean Douthat with our predicament. He understood our anxiety and tried to comfort us. Suddenly, he had an idea. He said that he would approach the fraternity council and make it a fraternity challenge. Again, our faith was being tested.

It just so happened that all of the leaders of the Greek social fraternities were meeting on campus that night. Mother, once again, turned to fasting and prayer. We placed our faith in God and trusted that His will would be manifested. We both prayed for another miracle.

The next morning, Dean Douthat met us with a smile. He said that following the fraternity meeting, two young men had stepped forward. They had never met me, but they had seen me on campus. Chip was from Michigan, and his father was a United States Congressman. "Q" was the son of a Florida shipping mogul and spent his summers sailing the Atlantic. Neither had ever taken care of anyone with a disability, but that did not matter. They were blessed with willing hearts and open minds. And they were both bigger than I was! They suggested that they would care for me one week and alternate weeks with two other students.

Our next challenge was to find another companionship. Again, Dean Douthat had an idea. He knew of a student, Jim, who, during the previous year, had worked to raise money for the Muscular Dystrophy Association. Mother literally ran across campus to the student's dormitory room! Her prayer had been answered, and she was fully acting to implement the Lord's answer. Jim was studious, brilliant, and eager to help. We just needed one more helper, and Jim knew of a friend, Rick, who might be interested.

Mother rushed to Rick's room down the hall. Rick was the polar opposite of Jim. Jim was conservative, philosophical, and reserved. By contrast, Rick appeared as though he had stepped out of the California surf. He was tanned and low-key, with hair down to his shoulders. He always wore a white T-shirt, jeans, and flip-flops.

Though he was from California, he appeared immune to the cold, damp winters in North Carolina.

With Rick's enlistment, my future at Duke was secure. From that small team of four helpers, there grew an army of helpers. By the time my mother left to return to Ohio in the latter part of October of 1974, she and I had acquired a network of fifty students pledged to help me attend Duke University! Each day and time slot was filled. Each meal was scheduled. There was someone to accompany me to each class. There was someone to walk to the library with me at night. There were others who would help shower and dress me each and every morning.

These were students who mainly came from very affluent backgrounds. They were at Duke University as a way of achieving their own goals and were intense and focused about their studies and the professions they would eventually pursue.

And yet, one by one, they answered the call. They were more than willing to help. They were always available to serve. They made room in their crowded lives for me. They were among the best and brightest. Still, they sacrificed and they loved me. And I still love them and will forever be grateful to them for helping me experience college life at Duke University.

There remained one last challenge. Neither Mother nor I wanted to face this change. The change was her having faith enough to say good-bye and to allow me the opportunity to be the college student that we had always hoped I would be. It was time for Mom to go home.

I never knew that change could be so painful. Mother was distraught. During all the other tough challenges and changes of my life, she had been there to comfort and strengthen me. Now she was not only sad, but appeared lost. She was so connected to me that she had never planned for what she would do once she no longer had to care for me.

For eighteen years, she had devoted herself to helping me survive. She had done everything that a mother can and should do to help her children. This change would be hard on me, but it was doubly hard for her. I could see it in her eyes and feel it in her embrace. As we said good-bye, we both sobbed. I felt sorry for her and felt the burden of her grief.

She then said, "We have raised you for this moment. You have always been a brave boy. Now it is time for you to shine. You know how much I don't want to leave you, but I must. I will miss you so much."

I was overcome with the feeling of gratitude for all she had done, all she had said, all she had taught me, and all she had meant to me—always.

I had never thanked her to the degree that she deserved. For the previous eighteen years I had been bathed, fed, held, taught, exhorted, and praised by this holy woman. I knew it, and I wanted her to know that I knew it. But words failed me. All I could repeat was, "I love you." She blew me kisses with her radiant smile as she closed the door behind her. Then I cried harder and longer than I ever had in my life.

CHAPTER SEVEN

"I AM JESUS CHRIST, WHOM THE PROPHETS TESTIFIED SHALL COME INTO THE WORLD"

With the physical demands of attending college so thoroughly addressed by Dean Douthat and Mom, I could turn my attention to my studies and devote more time and effort on what would be the direction of my life. In short, it was time to choose a major. In my first year, I was enthralled by two competing interests. Politics had always fascinated me, ever since my father had introduced me to the presidency and particularly to President Franklin D. Roosevelt.

During many hospitalizations and trying moments, Mom and I would often discuss the possibility of my running for public office one day. Such dreams of having a political career energized me and gave me the hope and desire to endure another day of pain and frustration. Thus, it was no surprise that I was intrigued by the study of political processes and issues or that I loved my Introduction to Political Science class.

Even though political science appeared to be a natural fit as a major, I was also drawn to the subject of religion. Duke was known for its Divinity School, which trained future ministers and preachers. The Divinity School faculty also featured world-renowned theologians, who not only taught graduate students but also offered undergraduate courses.

In my freshman year, I took a class on the New Testament taught by Professor James Charlesworth, who had worked on the project to translate and publish the Dead Sea Scrolls. His dynamic lectures introduced me to the compelling world of textual analysis, and I began studying the New Testament with an exciting perspective and applying new tools that deepened my understanding of the individual writers of the four Gospels and the messages they each taught.

In that class I also learned that the four Gospel writers had worked from a common source that contained the original words of Jesus. This was evident from the number of common phrases and teachings that appeared throughout the Gospels of Matthew, Mark, Luke, and John.

After taking Professor Charlesworth's class, I was faced with a dilemma. I had to choose which area of study would be my major. It was not an easy decision. One day I would conclude that I should choose political science, attend a law school, and pursue a political path. The next day, I would be convinced that I should become either a theologian or preacher. The pressure mounted as my indecision increased. Finally, I made a decision and elected to declare a double major in both political science and religion. It sounded unorthodox, but Dean Douthat reassured me that I was not the first student to double major in those subjects.

As my second-year studies developed, I was still comfortable with my choice of being a double major. However, my grades told a different story. Whereas I was excelling in my political science classes (receiving straight As), I was not so fortunate in my religion major. I had not garnered a single A in those courses and had managed only two straight Bs; my grade point average was suffering. I realized that I needed to improve my performance in my religion major or I would have to forsake my dream of graduating from Duke with a double major.

The fact is that grades matter, and if my sights were set on attending graduate school, no matter what the focus of my studies, I could not continue underperforming. Charitable as they may have been, Duke's religion professors were not known for their mercy and grace when it came to grades. They did not believe in bell curves, and special credit was something bestowed perhaps only after departing this life. Gratuitous grades were simply not awarded at the Duke Divinity School.

But I loved my religion classes, and I was unwilling to give up my second, and equally important, major. I searched desperately for a class that might provide me with some refuge from the storm of Bs that were bombarding my grade point average. Right as I was about to abandon my quest, I found my oasis in this academic desert.

The class was innocuously entitled, "Christianity in America." The synopsis sounded too good to be true: no exams, no quizzes, no classroom attendance taken, and no notes that needed to be taken during class—if and when you chose to attend class.

The only requirement for this particular religion class—completion of which virtually guaranteed every student with an A—was the successful completion of three, thirty-page papers on different topics with documented proof of a thousand pages of research for each paper. Christianity in America was no pushover; nothing at Duke ever was.

For my "easy A," I would have to submit at least ninety pages of papers for a single class in a single semester and prove in the bibliography at the end of each paper that I had actually researched a minimum of three thousand pages. But I desperately needed that A, and so I signed up, notwithstanding the treacherous mountain of paper that stood before me and the prize of a good grade at the summit.

Christianity in America was taught by Professor Barney Jones, a Methodist minister with captivating charm and an inviting smile. He was one of the most popular instructors at Duke; everyone loved Barney Jones.

I was at a loss as to what topic I should cover in my first thirty-page paper. Professor Jones provided a list of suggested topics. I settled on the eighteenth-century Anglican preacher, George Whitefield, who was credited with spreading "the Great Awakening" throughout Great Britain and America's colonies. The term, "Great Awakening," signifies several periods in British–American religious history in which there was a dramatic exchange of ideas and doctrines.

I was drawn to Whitefield for two reasons. First, I knew that Professor Jones greatly admired Whitefield's dynamic preaching. Second, I was intrigued by Whitefield's style of open-air preaching. When Whitefield traveled to America in the mid 1740s, he preached in mostly outdoor venues every day for months to large audiences that sometimes numbered in the thousands.

He traveled by horseback from New York to Charleston, which marked the longest trip by a Caucasian in American-Colonial history. The accounts of Whitefield's sermons and his oratorical skills reminded me of the Methodist minister at Duke's Chapel, Robert Young, whom I still consider to be one of the greatest orators I have ever heard. Researching Whitefield's work would be demanding due to the fact that Professor Jones was already intimately aware of Whitefield's biography and legacy.

I gladly received my A for the Whitefield paper. One thirty-page paper down, and only two more to go!

For my second paper topic, I wanted to do something that would be more alluring and fascinating than George Whitefield. I wanted a topic that was so compelling and so unique that Barney

Jones would remember my paper and me for a very long time. I wanted to impress him and my fellow classmates.

Once again I scoured the list of suggested topics that Jones had furnished for the class. None of them struck a chord. Nothing popped out as being unique enough to satisfy my strict criteria of being a subject that would simply enthrall my audience and me. And then suddenly my thoughts were turned toward my mother's religion, The Church of Jesus Christ of Latter-day Saints.

I realized that this class provided the golden chance for me to thoroughly research the beliefs that my mother espoused and the faith that was manifest from those beliefs. I concluded that I would never have such a chance to explore and study Mormon ideology and doctrine to this degree if I did not avail myself of this opportunity. I knew that I would most likely attend graduate school, which would demand so much effort and time that I would never be given another chance like this to come to terms with my mother's belief system. Now was the time and Duke was the place!

Up to that point, I was familiar with some of the broad contours that defined Mormonism. I was acquainted with the Book of Mormon as a focal point of the religion, but I had never read a single word contained within it. I did not recall my mother ever reading to me from the book during my hospitalizations.

I had also learned somewhat of Joseph Smith from my mother and had concluded from her explanation that he was a central figure in the restoration of the primitive religion that had been introduced by Jesus. I knew that Joseph Smith had claimed to have been called to form a new church after being visited by both God and Jesus Christ when he was a boy. I knew that he had said the event had taken place in a wooded area somewhere in Northeast America. However, I could not pinpoint such an event in time or location. I also knew that Mormons considered him a prophet, and yet the term "prophet" did not cause me any concern or compel me to research the ramifications of such a term further.

In short, for me, the Mormon religion was something that my mother associated herself with, and I had felt no pressure to come to any resolution about it. Mom had been a member of the Church since I was five years old. She still attended the Episcopal Church with our family, but I knew that on some Sundays, she would slip away and attend a small branch in a neighboring town.

I distinctly remember that Mother would return to us on those Sundays refreshed and rejuvenated. I never inquired why. I could just see that she was happier and more peaceful than when she attended church with us. She also seemed more inclined to share with us what had been discussed at these meetings. Again, I recalled nothing specific from her reports, but I remembered her enthusiasm and need to share information. She was clearly excited about what she had learned and was in the mood to teach us.

There was something else compelling me toward researching Mormonism. In spite of my disability, I never considered myself a sickly child, and yet I do recall missing school because of painful ear infections and incidents of the flu. In the 1960s, family physicians made house calls, and it was not unusual for my doctor to come to our home to examine me and recommend a certain course of treatment. I liked our family physician a lot and felt comfortable around him. But I did not always feel *comforted* by him.

Additionally, I had never felt any degree of empathy from the minister who would see me every Sunday when I sang in the combined boys and men's choir at the Episcopal Church. The prayer that he offered was always the same. It never seemed tailored to the specific situation that I found myself in. This was quite different from the prayers that my mother always offered on my behalf and the pattern of prayer that she had taught me.

I was not attracted to the rote prayers of the Episcopal Church. It never made sense to me that God would want His children to repeat the same prayer every Sunday or each time that they needed to communicate with him about their specific concerns and adversities.

But besides this logic, I could not forget the feeling I experienced every time I was sick and the Mormon missionaries would be summoned to our home by my mother to administer to me. I recall that they always came as soon as they could. They came with enthusiasm and sincerity. Most important, they came with a comforting power. Upon entering my room they would inquire as to what was ailing me. As they would talk to Mother and me, they were very engaged and eager to gather information. I remember always feeling comforted when Mother would announce, "I have called the missionaries to give you a blessing. They are on their way."

Unlike the predictable prayers of the Episcopal priest, the missionaries' prayers were specific, and the words they used were directed to God, whom they unfailingly addressed with reverence, gratitude, and humility.

The most significant thing from my early exposure to true priesthood power was when the missionaries would anoint my head with oil and pronounce a blessing of comfort and healing upon me. During those times, I felt a distinct power. I felt peaceful. I felt a closeness to God. I felt loved. When the missionaries would say, "God knows your condition and loves you," I believed them. It was more than a feeling. It was a witness.

The blessings always made my mother and me cry. But it was a good cry. It was a cry of relief and of rejoicing. I felt as though a burden was being lifted and that I would begin feeling better. I had faith in those early childhood blessings I received from humble missionaries who gladly and confidently placed their hands upon my head and blessed me with the spiritual gift of healing.

I could not forget the disappointment that I felt with my Episcopal priest. Coupled with this disappointment was my growing general apathy toward the Episcopal Church. The summer before I took the class on Christianity in America, I read a book about King Henry VIII. It was a bitter revelation to learn that I was a member of a church that had been founded by a serial adulterer. By the time I reached my sophomore year at Duke, I no longer felt any allegiance toward the Episcopal Church.

Although I was often emotionally moved by the minister at the Duke Chapel, Reverend Robert Young, and his soaring sermons, I was not interested in joining the Methodist Church.

I had always considered myself a spiritually inclined person, but I had not found a set of doctrines or ideology that I could attach myself to. I knew what I was not attracted to, but I did not know what I was searching for or even if I was searching.

I was a religion major and believed that I was a student of the New Testament. I had studied and analyzed practically every verse in it by the time I had enrolled in Barney Jones's class. I was confident in my beliefs, no matter how undefined those beliefs were. I believed in a God. I could not tell anyone with any degree of conviction what He looked like or where He was, and yet I could not deny that I had felt His power and His involvement in my life from a very early age.

I had studied Jesus from a historical perspective, but I did not feel any kinship with Him. I did not understand His role in my life, or if He even had any role in my life. At that point in my life, I considered Him a preacher, a miracle worker, and a prophet. The belief that He was resurrected had no impact on me from a spiritual perspective. My philosophy was theocentric—God and I had a relationship and that was all I knew and all I really cared about.

I did not subscribe to any particular beliefs in and about God or in and about Jesus Christ. But I did believe that God had created individuals and that each individual was free to believe in Him in whatever way that he or she deemed appropriate and functional for his or her needs. I was not particularly attracted to a religion that imposed its ideas about God on a community of so-called believers. In fact, I was opposed to it. At least, my mind was opposed to it.

That mental opposition and my definition of religion changed in the spring of 1976. Right before I began writing my paper about Mormonism, my mother paid me a visit. During her visit, we were strolling across campus back to my dormitory after she had picked me up at the library. It was a beautiful spring afternoon in North Carolina.

The subjects of religion and my beliefs were raised. I confidently declared, "Mom, God is a spirit. That is what it says in the New Testament."

Mother stopped me dead in my tracks. She stepped in front of my wheelchair and bent down so that our eyes met.

She had a simple, profound message to deliver: "Who are you to tell God who He is?"

I did not argue with her. How could I?

It was an unforgettable moment. She had raised me for a life of achievement, independence, and service. I was living out our dreams on the Duke campus. I knew she was proud of me. And I was proud of myself. But my pride was impairing my vision. She saw that I was relying on the arm of flesh to inform my spiritual belief system.

But none of my learning and achievements mattered when it came to pure doctrine and true religion and the testimony that she bore. She had no reservations or qualifications, no apologies or diplomacy. She was speaking from a platform of power and knowledge that was unavailable to me.

She was more confident than I, and I knew it; but most important, I felt it. I was humbled by her powerful witness. She had definitely challenged both my learning and my logic. And I had no reply.

So when I had the chance to choose a topic for my second paper,

I knew I needed to know more about her religion before it was too late. I could not forget what she had said or how it had made me feel. I needed to study the Mormon religion.

Thirty pages did not provide me the space to summarize this belief system. I needed to narrow my topic in order to make it more manageable and understandable to me and my audience.

There were a variety of topics from which I could choose to narrow my paper: Joseph Smith, the Mormon belief in a premortal life, a grand council being convened in heaven, and the subject of polygamy.

Certainly, all of these subjects were worthy of further study and exploration. But the one belief that I concluded was the most fantastic and sensational was the Mormon belief that Jesus had come to America following His death and resurrection in the Holy Land.

My first source for research references was, of course, just a phone call away. I telephoned Mom in Ohio and announced that the subject of my second paper was the Mormon proposition that Christ had visited America. I assured her that I was covering this topic in a very objective manner and was attracted to it only because it was so provocative.

Mother responded with enthusiasm, but not unbridled excitement. Dating back to her baptism in 1960, she was told not to place the Church before her family. She had been counseled that, in due time, her example and testimony would have such an effect that her entire family would come to accept the restored gospel of Jesus Christ.

In our telephone conversation she reminded me that she had conveniently placed a copy of the Book of Mormon on the bookshelf over my bed. Not surprisingly, she knew exactly where she had placed it. She told me that I would find the account of Christ's visit to America beginning in the book known as 3 Nephi. That struck me as a bit of a strange name, but I was grateful for her recommendations.

She also told me that there was another book that I would find useful, which was right beside the Book of Mormon. She said it was a small blue paperback by LeGrand Richards entitled *A Marvelous Work and a Wonder.*

I told her that I was going to check out every book possible on the subject so that I could present this topic in an impartial way for my professor. Mother wished me well, and I am convinced that she hung up the phone with her customary generous smile, realizing that my goal of objectivity would soon give way to a change brought on by the reference point of subjectivity that is contained within all of us—the Light of Christ!

When I went to the divinity school library, I took the cramped, darkened, and less-than-dependable elevator to the basement, which resembled an ancient tunnel system more than a library. It was dark and damp down there and always had a musty odor. I began dropping books one after another off the shelf onto my lap.

I found Sidney B. Sperry's *Commentary on the Book of Mormon.* I also discovered a dark blue hardback entitled *Jesus the Christ* by a man named James E. Talmage. There were a host of other books, some written by authors who I could tell from looking at the tables of contents had not been objective in their study of Mormonism. They were extremely critical and hostile in both their titles and tones. However, I desired objectivity; I read them as well.

I knew enough about Mormonism that I was aware that critics had called Joseph Smith a fraud and a charlatan and the religion that he had founded a cult or sect. But I had no stake in this religion. I was not offended by its opponents.

I was a sophomore at Duke who desperately needed an A grade in a religion class. Of course, I realized that this was the opportunity to come to terms with my mother's beliefs, but I was determined to write a thorough examination of the man Jesus, who came to

America following His alleged resurrection to meet and teach another population of believers known as Nephites. Almost instantly, as I began researching the Book of Mormon account of Christ's three-day visit in the Land Bountiful, I encountered a different type of Jesus. As a member of the Episcopal Church, I had studied Jesus in the New Testament and had learned about Him and His teachings. But I had always believed that He was a largely misunderstood and harassed miracle worker. I felt that He was forced to rely on parables in order to reach true believers, but those parables never had much relevance to me and my life. He was unappreciated and persecuted. From the accounts in the four Gospels, there appeared to be very few converts. Even two of His most loyal followers, Peter and Judas—counted from among His own twelve disciples—failed Him at the end of His ministry.

This was not the case in the Book of Mormon. Here, Jesus spoke with power and clarity. He taught doctrines that were understandable and cogent. He explained His life and its purpose as never before. Equally impressive to me was the fact that His audience not only listened to Him, but they heard Him. They understood Him. They had been waiting for Him. And most important, this audience did not attack Him, but rather adored and worshipped Him.

Up until that point, I had always felt sorry for Jesus. I could not understand why there were so many detractors and people who ignored Him or rebuked Him, as recounted in the Gospels. I was astonished that His own people had not only labeled Him a rebel and heretic but also had manufactured spurious charges of treason against Him. I was dismayed that these people whom He had come to save had chosen Barabbas to live and had applauded when He was nailed to the most crude and inhumane implement of death. It had never made any sense.

But the Jesus who taught the Nephite nation was both strong

and understood. There were no apologies, no hidden agendas, and no disappointments or dissensions. No confusion. No doubt. No betrayals. No sadness.

I read the riveting account of this Jesus, who wept not because He was paying the price of our sins, but because He, at last, had found joy, and it made Him full.

The Nephite audience listened intently for hours. They could not get enough. They worshipped Him and hung on His every word. This account not only captivated me, but fascinated me. It was as if I were among those masses that greeted Him and beheld the wounds that He allowed each individual to see and feel. This was the Jesus I had been waiting for and had never found—until now. There He was in His glorified, resurrected state, teaching as only He could and loving as only He could. He was not only a captivating figure; He was indeed the Messiah. King of Kings. Lord of Lords. He was the Savior and Redeemer of the world. And I had found Him!

I knew it! Suddenly this was no ordinary assignment. I was in pursuit of something much more important than an A. I was discovering the truth and meaning of life. It was as if I were remembering something that I had always known but had somehow forgotten when I came to this earth. It all made sense. I felt it. I believed it.

The more I read, the more I was convinced that the account of Jesus in America truly happened. But it was so much more. I was knocking at the door of a new mansion that was overflowing with knowledge and light.

I spent long hours alone as I read and wrote about the Mormon Jesus. I was cloistered inside a tiny room that featured only one table and a safe that contained ancient Egyptian papyri. Each sentence I wrote was punctuated by a feeling that I believed what I was writing. But I wanted a manifestation of the Spirit confirming to me that this church was restored through the Prophet Joseph Smith and that the promise in Moroni 10:4 was valid:

> And when ye shall receive these things, I would exhort you that ye would ask God, the Eternal Father, in the name of Christ, if these things are not true; and if ye shall ask with a sincere heart, with real intent, having faith in Christ, he will manifest the truth of it unto you, by the power of the Holy Ghost.

And so as I studied and wrote, I also prayed for a burning in my bosom. I did not want a gentle whisper in my soul; I sought something more dramatic. And I did receive an answer, yet I initially dismissed it as being simply a wish or desire. But that was only my own denial and fear of adopting a new way of life.

My anxieties soon disappeared, however, when it was time to present my paper to my classmates, who received it with visible discomfort and skepticism. Professor Barney Jones joined them in their hostile comments.

But that did not discourage me; it only persuaded me that what I had presented to them was true. It emboldened me to press forward and continue my research. I received an A on my paper, but I had received much more than a grade. I had studied Jesus in America for my Christianity in America class, and my witness of Him as the Christ was emerging. My conversion had commenced.

It was the summer of 1976, and I was going to Washington, D.C., to intern for a United States congressman. I was excited to have such an opportunity, but once again my parents and I faced the logistical challenges of where I would live and who would take care of me during the summer. Mother knew just what I needed. My father found an apartment in Annandale, Virginia, and Mother contacted the bishop of the ward.

The bishop said that he knew of a young man who had just returned from his mission in Peru and was looking for work. I had met missionaries before, but I had never known a Mormon who was my age before I met Reed Whitlock. While I was writing my paper at Duke, I had encountered a couple of missionaries on campus and invited them to teach me, but after the first lesson, I told them that I had studied enough Mormonism and that I felt I needed time alone without unnecessary pressure. I was still trying to absorb and evaluate all of the information that had challenged my religious belief system. I needed to think about things. Now I refer to such thinking as *pondering* and *meditating*.

Reed Whitlock was the perfect fit to care for me. I could relate to him. He loved politics. He had a sarcastic sense of humor. And although he did not major in religion, it was obvious that Reed understood the scriptures better than I did. And he was not the only one.

On the first Sunday that I attended the Annandale Ward, I was humbled to hear of the knowledge that so many members freely imparted. There was no arrogance in their simple expressions of faith. Everyone had an opinion, but no one seemed to be threatened by anyone else. The people were sincere and genuine, and I felt comfortable. I felt as if I belonged to this community of believers.

The summer of 1976 was also America's Bicentennial, and it seemed as though every day there was a new event in Washington commemorating America's 200th birthday. On the Fourth of July, I attended a meeting of Latter-day Saints at the Capitol Centre, a sports arena in Landover, Maryland. Mom called the meeting a devotional. The Mormon Tabernacle Choir performed. At the time, it was the largest meeting of Mormons outside of Utah in the history of the Church. I do not remember any of the songs or the content of any of the sermons. But I do remember the reaction of the crowd when a certain diminutive man walked onto the stage. There was absolute silence and reverence for him.

I remember he spoke with a distinct, raspy voice, which was amplified by a microphone attached to his ear. I cannot tell you what he talked about on that day, but I cried through his entire sermon, and I knew that he was no ordinary man. Mormons considered him their prophet, seer, and revelator. His name was Spencer W. Kimball, and I felt the power and authority with which he spoke. It was an undeniable feeling that had overcome my heart. I left that arena knowing that I had sat at the feet of a prophet.

On August 4, 1976, Reed Whitlock carried me in his arms into a font and baptized me by immersion. With Mother, Dad, and my sister Carole looking on, he afterwards confirmed me a member of The Church of Jesus Christ of Latter-day Saints.

It is impossible to describe the degree of pure joy that I saw on my mother's face the evening of my baptismal service. She was more than happy. She was beaming with gratitude and thrilled with the realization that I now had a witness of those things that she knew were true. Those truths, which had supported her and guided her in taking care of me since I was five years old, were now an integral part of who I was. It is hard to imagine, but my decision to be baptized made our bond as mother and son even stronger. We both felt it, and we both knew it.

At the beginning of that year, all I had desired was the gift of a good grade for my resume. But then I received the boundless gifts of the Holy Ghost and the priesthood. And I still sit all amazed at the love Jesus offers me!

CHAPTER EIGHT

"HE WILL TAKE
UPON HIM THE PAINS
AND THE SICKNESSES
OF HIS PEOPLE"

I graduated from Duke with high honors and was admitted to Brigham Young University's Law School. I was eager to be associated with Latter-day Saints, since there were not many of us at Duke. In fact, there were only five out of five thousand! In the ward I attended outside the Duke campus, I was blessed to have Stephen Robinson—author of *Believing Christ*—as my first Gospel Doctrine teacher. Brother Robinson was a theology graduate student at the Duke Divinity School at the time, and his gospel understanding and exceptional teaching ability had a profound influence on me in those early months of my membership in the Church.

When I arrived in Provo, I reveled in the opportunity to learn more about the gospel. It was an exciting time for me spiritually.

I was also studying at a great law school. I was one of the youngest males in my class. In fact, most of the other students had served missions and were already married by the time they reached that particular academic level. My courses were demanding, and it was a

Graduation day from Duke University, 1978.
Carole, Grandfather, me, and Mildred.

competitive environment, but I was thrilled to be preparing for my career as an attorney.

I loved my student ward. I lived off campus in a sprawling apartment complex. Although I was studying at the same pace that I had established at Duke, which allowed for one night off per week, I still had a social life. I fell in love more than once, but my desire to get married was not reciprocated. And, yet, my mother had once promised me that I would meet someone very special, and I held out hope that her words would come to fruition.

While in law school, I spent my summers as a law clerk for Senator Orrin Hatch (R.-Utah) in Washington, D.C.

After graduating from law school, I was hired as an assistant attorney general for the State of Utah. It is not surprising that the private sector was devoid of possibilities; not many law firms were interested in taking on a disabled applicant who could guarantee only that he could work forty hours per week. But I acknowledged my limitations and offered no apology. I was thankful to not only have a job, but to have landed a great job.

*With my parents, January 1983, after I was sworn
in at the Utah Supreme Court.*

During my first three years of practice, I made more than forty appearances before the Utah Supreme Court. Arguing a case before five Supreme Court justices is a daunting experience, especially when they are bound and determined to interrupt you mid-sentence with questions to test the strength and limits of your argument. I had the added pressure of knowing that if I failed and lost a case, a convicted felon, serving his sentence at the Utah State Prison, would be set free or at least be given a new trial. That is pressure and stress!

But I was blessed with the gift of being a good debater, and I relished this intellectual tug of war. I felt liberated not having to study every night, and I spent weekends with my sister Carole, her husband, Neil, and their first daughter, Jennifer.

Of course, life was not without its challenges and setbacks. But I encountered nothing unique in any of the hurdles or distractions I faced. There was the ongoing need to recruit dependable helpers to assist me in my morning and evening routine. That necessity had not changed dramatically from my days at Duke when Mother and Dean Douthat had helped provide it.

I was happy and I was content. But this period of relative calm and comfort ended suddenly and unexpectedly, and it was horrifying.

———⟪❦⟫———

It began in January 1986. Carole had just given birth to her second baby, Caitlin. Mother came out to help, but she was uncharacteristically listless, confused, and even indifferent about the new baby and providing support and assistance to Carole. Given her usual energy level and devotion to her family, it was so inexplicable to see her demonstrate no concern or motivation. She looked as though she were moving in slow motion.

One incident was truly alarming. She telephoned Carole and told her she would meet Carole at her house that morning. But she did not arrive until afternoon, which was highly uncharacteristic. My mother, especially when it came to her children, was on time and on task. It had always been that if we needed her, we merely had to ask. In fact, most of the time, she anticipated our needs and simply did what was necessary. That no longer seemed to be the case.

When she finally arrived at Carole's home, she offered no explanation for her late arrival, except that she had lost track of time. That did not sound remotely like our mother. It was as if she had discarded her customary and unparalleled nurturing spirit and taken on a new, alien personality.

Rather than help out, Mother was content to rest on Carole's couch. In an effort to arouse some sort of interest, Carole suggested that Mother go to a nearby strip mall and help three-year-old Jennifer buy a goldfish.

What should have been a brief trip down the street became an hour-long ordeal. When Mother and Jennifer finally returned home, Mother appeared dazed and disoriented. Jennifer remarked,

"Mommy, Grammy Mikita got lost, and I had to tell her where to drive us to get back home." Something was obviously very wrong. Jennifer had found her goldfish, but Mother was clearly lost.

None of us could understand what was happening to our mother. We questioned our father for answers, but he dismissed Mom's behavior as probably a little seasonal depression. But that was much too simplistic, not to mention inaccurate.

Mother returned to Ohio the next day. Mom and Dad would be leaving for their annual visit to Palm Springs for a few weeks, and Dad thought that the sun and warmth of the desert would buoy her spirits.

At the beginning of the week, I telephoned home to check on her. The phone rang at least twenty times. Finally, a very faint voice answered.

I immediately said, "Mom, what are you doing?"

She said, "I am sleeping."

I said, "Why are you sleeping?"

She said, "I am tired."

I said, "Mom, do you know what time it is?"

She said, "No."

I responded, "It is noon."

Mom then said, "Well, I better get up and start packing. We leave for Palm Springs tomorrow."

I said, "Mom, you don't leave for Palm Springs tomorrow."

She said, "Oh. What day is it?"

With fear marking every word, I said, "Mom, you don't know what day it is? I am going to call Dad. I love you."

I was still in shock as I dialed the number to my father's office. I told his secretary that I needed to speak with him urgently and that even though he was consulting with a patient, she needed to interrupt him.

When Dad picked up the phone, I recited what had transpired. I pleaded with him to do something. I said, "Dad, something is terribly wrong with Mom. You've got to help her. Please cancel the trip and take her to a psychiatrist. She is really, truly disoriented and depressed."

Dad replied, "Okay, I will cancel the trip and take her to a psychiatrist in Pittsburgh."

From that moment on, the news went from bad to worse. Following an examination by a psychiatrist, Mother was diagnosed as severely depressed and contemplating suicide.

I could not grasp those words. I could not conceive of my mother ever wanting to take her life. She had always had so much to live for and so much left to give to her family—especially to her grandchildren—and to the Church. In my opinion, she would be the last person on earth who would ever entertain such a thought. I felt as if I had been struck by lightning. My mother was actually considering suicide? I could not understand what was unraveling in her life that would lead her to such dark thoughts. Dad conceded that he did not know and that the psychiatrist, at this point, did not know, either.

Dad informed me that he would need to bring Mom home for a couple of days until the psychiatric hospital had a bed available for her. He assured me that he was going to take every precaution to protect her until she could get to the hospital.

I was engulfed by horrible images that I could not purge from my mind. Nothing made any sense. After hanging up the phone, I rolled my wheelchair in front of a collage of photographs that hung on one of my bedroom walls. My eyes were immediately drawn to a photograph of my parents and me that had been taken at a beach in Delaware a couple of years before. My mother's signature smile and love for life that she had imparted to all of her children was clear to see.

As I looked at her smiling face, I sensed that what was happening was something more than depression; something was killing her, and I wept because I knew that from that time forward our relationship on earth would never be the same. Although her doctors did not yet know it, I knew it, and I had received a witness that my conclusion was correct. Our roles would be reversed; I would have to be the strong one for her now. I would have to be the one to raise her spirits and give her hope and strengthen her faith, as she had done for me.

That night, I began grieving the pending death of my mother.

I telephoned her the next morning and was met with the same quiet monotone voice that had greeted me for the last several weeks. My mantra did not change. I would say, "Mom, I love you. Life is still worth living. You need to fight. Don't give up. You are going to be okay. I am praying for you."

I could tell that there was a barrier to our communication. She was hearing me but not actually comprehending the words I was speaking. An impenetrable wall had grown between us.

Once she entered the hospital, Mother's condition rapidly deteriorated. She became increasingly incoherent, confused, and disoriented. She did not know where she was and would claim that she had not seen Dad for weeks. She was not participating in therapy sessions and preferred to sleep instead. In my telephone calls to her, she would offer one-word, meaningless responses. I could tell she did not know who I was and could not respond to my questions.

Finally, after ten days of just observing her, the doctors ordered that Mother undergo a CAT scan. The results were astonishing. Carole and I were visiting when Dad called to give us the shocking news.

Carole picked up the phone and then exclaimed, "Dear God, no!" She looked at me in utter amazement and said, "Stevie, Mom has been diagnosed with a brain tumor. She only has six weeks to live."

Once again, it was as if time stood still. I could not focus on what was being said. I was in shock and denial. This was my worst nightmare; my mother was dying.

For most of us, the greatest fear in our lives is the loss of a loved one. Parents fear the loss of a child or grandchild. Siblings fear the loss of a brother or sister. Spouses fear the death of their partners.

My greatest fear, however, was that I would outlive my mother. She had come from such a healthy lineage that my father would often quip, "Mom is going to outlive all of us." While growing up, I just knew Dad was right.

I was the one who had received all the predictions of an early death, and it was my mother's love and faith to which I clung during every crisis and painful ordeal. She had been there through it all; she was my rock, and I could not conceive of living my life without her.

I had always assumed that I would die before she would. Now that equation had been erased from my life. Mother was dying; she was leaving me before I was leaving her! I felt so alone, so vulnerable, and so sorrowful! We were a team, after all. I had never endured any trial without her by my side. That was the only way I had survived, let alone thrived.

Through my trials, I had always told myself that I could endure anything and everything, so long as Mom was there to support me and watch over me. We had fought every fight and enjoyed every triumph together as mother and son. And now that was being taken away from me.

How could I go on without her? How could this be happening?

Why was she being taken away? What had I done to deserve this? These were questions to which I had no answers.

I became resentful. Hadn't I hung on during the tough times? Hadn't I acknowledged God's hand and mercies in my life?

I knew how richly my life had been blessed. I always acknowledged my abundant life and strived to live in a way that could somehow reciprocate all that I had been given and all that I had learned about God and His plan. But this—my mother's impending death—I could not understand. I didn't want to. Nothing had prepared me for this harsh reality. This trial was much too bitter to swallow. This tragedy was much too ironic to accept. This loss was much too painful to ask me to endure.

What would my life be without her? What would be the purpose of the future without sharing it with her by my side? Who would I talk to? Who would comfort me? Who would be my champion? Who would be my refuge? Who would hold my hand and wipe my tears? Who would lift me when I fell? Who would rescue me when I was lost?

Who?

CHAPTER NINE

"PEACE I LEAVE WITH YOU, MY PEACE I GIVE UNTO YOU"

I was alone, but I had not been forgotten. I was in pain, but I was not without relief. I was sad, but not bereft. I was lost, but I had the faith that somehow I would be rescued. Although I was living my worst nightmare and seeing it unfold day by day, there was a calm peace that finally enveloped me. There was a presence. There was a Spirit. There was comfort. There was God.

As I sat alone one night after I had heard the awful news that my mother was dying, I returned once again to the photograph of my mother's beaming smile. An undeniable feeling swept over me. A feeling of understanding. The source of the feeling came not from a distance or remote place; it was immediate and proximate. It was very near, very aware, and very present. It was as if it was right there and I could touch it; it was that real and tangible.

I realized at that moment that I was not alone. I would not have to carry this burden and this loss by myself. I couldn't carry it. I

With my mother, March 1987, six months
before she passed away.

didn't want to carry it. The weight of my grief was too heavy, and I was too weak. I was too scared.

But I felt understood. I felt reassured. I felt as though someone cared about what I was being asked to go through. I recognized that God was beside me.

Although Mother survived for almost twenty months with her brain tumor, I did not doubt during that time that God was involved in my life and was aware of what I was going through. He knew how much I loved my mother. He knew how much I needed her. He knew how much she meant to me. He sustained me as I came to grips with her passing.

I trusted that God also knew how much I meant to my mother. He knew how much she would miss me. He knew the extent of her efforts to nurture and care for me. He knew how much joy she experienced from seeing my accomplishments. He knew how much she wanted to live a long life for her children and grandchildren, and to serve Him and His Son.

It is my testimony that He not only knew about how I felt and how my mother felt, but He knew it *perfectly.* God knew me, and He knew her.

I wanted her to stay with me and live a longer life on earth. She wanted the same thing. But neither my plan nor her plan was His plan, and I needed to acquiesce to His wisdom.

It surprised me that I wasn't angry or bitter. Instead, I was humbled and willing to submit to His will and His plan. I knew, but needed to be reminded, that the Lord's plan is overflowing with His perfect love and perfect awareness of what we need and when we need it.

Somehow, I opened my heart to receive His love, and I felt it. I felt blessed. The Holy Ghost performed His promised duty in comforting me. I had faith in God's love for and knowledge of me. Though my faith and understanding had been expanded by receiving a testimony of the restored gospel, the foundation of that faith had been laid by my mother. It was she who first planted in my heart the belief that God lives, that He loves us, that He is mindful of us, and that He hears and answers our prayers. This new and unwanted situation helped me more fully live in the shining light of the restored gospel of Jesus Christ.

I had assimilated the doctrines intellectually; now it was time to internalize them—in the face of the raw emotions that mortality brings to each one of us.

It was not easy to do. There were many tears and much pain as my mother's disease progressed. When I would talk to my mother on the telephone, I felt restrained from telling her what was really bothering me. Even with the pressure on her brain and the resulting incoherence that it produced much of the time, she still discerned that I was preoccupied and not telling her my honest feelings during our discussions.

She would often ask, "Honey, what's the matter?"

I would reply, "I just get scared."

She would ask, "What are you afraid of?"

I would say, "I just don't want you to be afraid, Mom."

Then she would say, "Oh, I'm not afraid. I'm the mother of a brave little boy who taught me about courage and not to fear."

Even in the midst of her greatest trial, my mother reminded me of who I was and in whose arms I was still embraced.

In August 1987, I traveled back to Ohio; I did not know it, but this would be the last time that I would see my mother alive. She spent most of the time I was there sleeping in her hospital bed located in what had once been my bedroom. When she was awake, she was agitated and called out constantly for my father. He had an intercom next to his chair in the living room so he could hear her movements and calls for assistance.

She would merely have to say his name, "Bill," and he would immediately leap to his feet and sprint up the winding staircase to the bedroom. His devotion never wavered. Every time she would call, he would respond as if it were the first time. Even though he was sixty-five-years old, he would run up the stairs and say, "Okay, doll, here I come. What do you need?"

On the weekend I was there, I stopped counting how many times he responded to my mother's calls. He never became impatient or demonstrated any irritation at her frequent summons. His willingness to serve her was an inspiring testament to their eternal bond.

When we were children, Dad would often remark, "The greatest gift that a father can give his children is the knowledge that he loves their mother." His belief in that axiom was never more clearly and powerfully demonstrated than on that weekend I spent with both of them. I saw a tangible evidence of my father's love for my mother each time he would climb the stairs. Seeing my father care for my mother is indelibly etched into my heart.

But then, it was time to say good-bye. I rolled my wheelchair into her room and reached for her familiar hand that had been my anchor through so many storms. We had faced so many trials together that it was painful for me to say, "Mom, I have to go now. But I don't want to. I just want to stay here and hold your hand."

She smiled and said, "You have to go. You have to become that man that I raised you to become."

All I could think to say was, "I love you, Mom." And then I let go of her precious hand.

<center>~~~⚬~~~</center>

By September 13, 1987, Mother had lapsed into a coma and was lying in a hospital room. Dad telephoned Carole and me and told us to get on the first plane back to Ohio—things were deteriorating rapidly.

That evening, before we left Salt Lake City, I telephoned the hospital room, and my sister Judy answered. Judy said Mom was pretty unresponsive, but I asked if she could put the telephone up against Mother's ear.

When she placed the phone up to Mother, I said, "Mom, this is Stevie."

Immediately, the pattern of her breathing became much more frequent and rapid. She knew who she was hearing.

I told her, "It is time for you to let go and return home to Heavenly Father. I don't want you to hang on anymore just for me. Carole will take care of me here in Utah. I do not want you to worry. I love you so much. I will see you soon."

Judy got back on the phone. She confirmed that Mother's breathing had changed and that she had definitely recognized my voice.

The next morning, I was on a plane flying back to Ohio. It was a beautiful, serene morning over the Rocky Mountains of Wyoming when, in spite of my fear of flying, I inexplicably began falling asleep. Twice I was startled from my slumber by a blinding light, which I assumed came from outside the windows of the aircraft. But the third time the shaft of exquisite light reappeared, I heard a voice.

The voice simply said, "Stevie."

It was a happy voice.

It was a healthy voice.

It was a familiar voice.

It was Mom's voice.

Three and a half hours later, when the plane landed in Pittsburgh, my brother, Billy, boarded the plane to help me. I asked him if I had made it in time, but his moistened eyes answered me before he uttered a word. He said, "No, Steve, Mom died this morning."

I asked, "What time did she die?"

Billy said, "Eleven-thirty A.M., Eastern Daylight Time."

I remembered the scene on the aircraft. It was 9:30 A.M. over the mountains of Wyoming when I saw that brilliant shaft of light and heard my mother's unmistakable, clear, and precious voice speak my name.

That was yet another precious assurance that neither my mother nor God had abandoned me. I was not alone, even though my grief was overwhelming.

I noted in chapter 7 that until I came in contact with The Church of Jesus Christ of Latter-day Saints and its teachings I had only a limited understanding of the importance of Jesus in the plan of salvation. Since my conversion and baptism, I have come to know and love Him as my personal Savior and Redeemer. Here are some of the things I now know about Him.

One of the most beautiful and powerful aspects of the Atonement of Jesus Christ is the depth of His compassion for each of us. His Atonement not only paid the price for our sins and our transgressions, so long as we repent and come to Him with a broken heart and contrite spirit, but, equally important, His sacrifice and experience in the Garden of Gethsemane provided Him the path to feel and experience every loss and grief that you and I will ever experience.

When Jesus trembled because of pain, when he bled from every pore, suffering in both body and spirit, He not only satisfied the demands of justice, but I believe His body was filled with boundless mercy and love for each one of us.

Consequently, He understands all of us and what we are asked to endure. He is not an idle, disinterested spectator. He invites us to come to Him for healing, understanding, and unmatched love and power. It is His power, not ours, that can overcome any trial that we face. He took upon Himself our afflictions and trials and He is never too busy to help us. We merely have to ask and rely on Him. For His yoke is easy and His burden is light.

Jesus did not live with a neuromuscular disease, but I know He understands every pain, every ordeal, every anguish, every setback, every disappointment, and every rejection that I have experienced while living my life with such a disease. He understands me more perfectly and loves me more powerfully than anyone, including my beloved mother. I see now that He has been beside me every step of the way. He is always ready to strengthen me and help me to carry on, no matter how difficult the trial, no matter how excruciating the pain.

Jesus did not die of cancer or any other disease or condition that might afflict any one of us. But that does not mean He does not understand perfectly—in every minute detail—the pain, despair, and fear of those who have been struck by dreadful diseases. He also understands the grief, sorrow, and helplessness of those of us who sit at the bedsides of our loved ones and who, in such moments, ask, "Why not me? How can this family go on without him or her? Why has God forsaken me or us?"

He not only understands the questions, but His overpowering love and indescribable compassion and mercy will, in time, answer every one of those seemingly unanswerable questions. He is Alpha and Omega. He sees the beginning and the end. He is at once the Master of the universe and the unfailing Shepherd of His flock.

Jesus was not abused by his parents. But He understands in every way and every aspect the feelings that children have and continue to experience in enduring these horrifying crimes. He knows all. He has felt it all. He has overcome it all—not for Himself, but for us! He took all of it upon Himself so that He could comfort us and rescue us in the darkest moments and in the terrifying gardens that we must pass through ourselves.

Jesus did not suffer from any addiction. But through the Atonement, He is full of compassion and mercy for anyone who is tempted by any dependency or codependency. He is the ultimate and highest power available to overcome. He has, in some miraculous way, already overcome the most harrowing and controlling feelings of addiction that anyone has ever been, or ever will be, subjected to by the adversary's arsenal. The devil has no control over Him.

Consequently, those who struggle with and sincerely commit to defeating the demons of addiction can only overcome by leaning on the power and love of Him who first overcame. We cannot do it alone. He is there not only to listen to us and empathize with us, but also to eventually and definitively silence the temptations; to defeat, once and for all, the cravings.

Jesus did not witness one of His children die during His earthly ministry. But He understands the terror and continuing grief of every parent, everywhere, no matter the circumstance, of those who lose one of their little ones. He is there to hear, help, and heal the deepest of wounds.

Jesus did not have a wayward son or daughter. But He understands and feels the anxiety, grinding concern, and moments of hopelessness that every parent experiences with a child who is either apathetic toward, or opposed to, God's plan of happiness.

He absolutely feels what we feel because He experienced it first.

Jesus understands the pain and loneliness of single adults who, through no fault of their own, have not found their eternal companions. His love and compassion extends to those of us who are unmarried and who experience hours and even days of longing and yearning for that special someone to share our lives with. Though we are single in this life, we are still linked inextricably and eternally to Him. He is there to help us as we watch and wait and, if necessary, wait some more. He knows, and will ultimately bless us for, the righteous desires of our hearts. He knows each of us by name. He never stops caring for or comforting us. His love knows no time, no boundary, no age, and no status. We are His. And He is ours.

Jesus is more than simply aware of parents who have been called to care for special-needs children. He knows of their tireless commitment and sacrifice. He has felt their fatigue and exhaustion.

How can He know this? How can He feel it? Does He still truly care about me and you?

Depression may be invisible to many of us. But it is a real diagnosis, and Jesus knows the devastating impact of depression on those who suffer from this illness:

And they came to a place which was named Gethsemane: and he saith to his disciples, Sit ye here, while I shall pray.

And he taketh with him Peter and James and John, and began to be sore amazed, and to be very heavy;

And saith unto them, My soul is exceeding sorrowful unto death: tarry ye here, and watch.

And he went forward a little, and fell on the ground, and prayed that, if it were possible, the hour might pass from him. (Mark 14:32–35)

As Elder Neal A. Maxwell explained, "Mark wrote that Jesus became 'sore amazed' and 'very heavy' (Mark 14:33), meaning in the Greek, respectively, 'astonished and awestruck' and 'depressed and dejected.' None of us can tell Christ anything about depression!" (Maxwell, "Enduring Well," 10).

For the innocent victims of sexual crimes and violence, He is also there. He has not forgotten you. He has not forgotten the monstrous perpetrators of those crimes, and He will sit as the Ultimate Judge. If you are innocent, your integrity will not be attacked, and your character will not be impugned. All will be made right in His time and under His perfect laws. He is your Advocate with the Father. He understands all of it, every bit of it. His defense of your rights never ends, and His demands for retribution will be satisfied. In the meantime, He invites us to cast our cares upon Him and allow Him to treat our emotional scars with the healing tears He has already cried on our behalf. He still remembers us from the Garden.

We need not fear. We need not doubt. We need only to believe in and rely on Him.

Behold, this is the promise of the Lord unto you, O ye my servants.

Wherefore, be of good cheer, and do not fear, for I the Lord am with you, and will stand by you; and ye shall bear record of me, even Jesus Christ, that I am the Son of the living God, that I was, that I am, and that I am to come. (D&C 68:5–6)

The great Apostle Paul stated, "For God hath not given us the spirit of fear; but of power, and of love, and of a sound mind" (2 Timothy 1:7).

As for me, I cannot stand, but He stands beside me. I cannot kneel, but He hears my prayers before I have said a word. I cannot wipe my tears, but He wipes them for me because He has already tasted the salt on my cheeks.

He wipes away all of our tears. He has faced all of our fears. He loves us. That is my testimony!

CHAPTER TEN

"THAT YOUR JOY MIGHT BE FULL"

In a recent discussion with a close friend, the topic of pressing forward despite troubling times surfaced. She remarked, "How is it that you are able to be so optimistic when year after year your muscles become weaker? We have known each other for quite a long time, and I remember when you were able to do so much more. I remember when you were able to feed yourself, sign your name to your checkbook or on a credit card receipt, hold a telephone up to your ear, dial a telephone, and shake people's hands. There was a time when you could be left alone at your home for three- or four-hour spans and not have your personal care staff constantly around you. You had privacy. You had independence. You had control. You had abilities and skills."

I laughed and said to my friend, "Can you give me another bite of my meal now that it is cold? Then I will answer you!"

I began by reminding her of my perspective on where I had been and where I am going. I have never spent much time dwelling on the

With my sister Carole and her husband, Neil,
and Utah Jazz basketball player Karl Malone
at a 1993 fundraiser that I held for children
with my same muscle disease.

abilities and skills that were once mine but are no longer available to me. To be candid, I do not remember them in precise detail. It seems as though so much effort goes into living day to day and maintaining my health and meeting my needs that I do not have much time to reflect on what I used to be able to do and how I was able to do it. I am more concerned about what I have to do today and what is on my agenda for tomorrow.

As a matter of fact, I do not greatly miss the things that I used to be able to do to the degree that one might initially think. Fortunately, my body has gone through a subtle, gradual decline. For example, throughout the years I went from holding a fork in my right hand to eat as most individuals do, to holding the fork in my left hand, to adopting a two-handed technique in order to adapt as my fingers, hands, and arms became less and less cooperative. Eventually, the adaptations were exhausting, and I was ready to accept the reality that I could no longer feed myself. I was prepared to move forward to the next phase of my life of being fed by others and concentrating instead on instructing my family and helpers on the types of bites and the pace of bites that I found satisfying.

"I have very little control over the progression of my disease," I explained to my friend. "But I have a lot of control over my *reaction* to the progression of my disease." Having lived for five decades with a muscle disease has provided me with ample proof that sooner or later, my body is destined to fail me. But what won't fail me is my attitude, my family, my friends, and my Savior. Those are the things and the people I can count on and trust. Those are the things that fill my life with hope, happiness, and strength.

Of course I experience frustrations and losses just like everyone else. There are very discouraging moments and even days that I would just as soon not have to endure, let alone experience. But though I would prefer to avoid them, that is not part of the plan. It is, after all, not my plan, and it is not under my control.

My friend was not easily persuaded. She said, "Surely you must get depressed. How could you not?"

Relieved that I could take a quick bite before answering her, I said, "I once asked a friend whether she thought I was depressed. She said, 'I don't know whether you are depressed; you have to diagnose that part for yourself.'

"I asked, 'What do you mean?'

"She explained, 'Well, let me ask you a question. Do you feel depressed?'

"I said, 'Sometimes I feel sadness or loneliness.'

"She asked a new question. 'Do you have any joy in your life?'

"As I thought about that, tears welled up in my eyes, and I said, 'There is not a single day in which I do not experience some joy.'

"She asked, 'What do you mean by that?'

*Enjoying Easter, 1990, with Carole's girls, Caitlin
(four years old) and Jennifer (seven years old).*

"I told her, 'Well, even though I may be getting physically weaker, or I may have a frustrating case at work, or I may be worried about a relationship or the health of a loved one, I still feel joy on a daily basis. That might not last the entire day, but there are parts of each day that I find or feel or am touched by joy.'"

That is absolutely the truth. There may be only fleeting moments on a particularly difficult day, but happiness that comes by way of knowing who we are and by understanding the intimate involvement of our Heavenly Father in our lives should touch each of us at a certain moment of every day and cause us to rejoice. We are loved. We are understood. And the evidence of that love and of that understanding is shown to us through the love of family members and friends. These moments of joy are not an illusion. For me, they exist, and they are real.

That does not mean that every day I want to shout for joy from the rooftop that my life is overflowing with unbridled joy. That is not what I am talking about. To think that such would be the case is

The Mikita children, Christmas 1960.

inconsistent with the Lord's teaching that you and I will experience tribulation. But it is because of Him that joy is attainable each and every day, wherever we find ourselves and whatever we are experiencing.

I wanted to provide my friend some examples of what I was referring to, so I said, "There are a lot of things that bring me joy. It is very rare that I do not laugh during the day in response to a comment made by a colleague or friend or even me. Laughter brings me great joy. Humor does make a difference in our lives. One cannot live a full life without being touched by life's ironies and comedies. Being able to laugh at one's self or at life's paradoxical turns makes every day more enjoyable."

Another great source of joy, I explained, is my family. One of the greatest blessings in my life is the eternal bond that I have with my siblings, Carole, Bill, and Judith. Carole and I both live in Salt Lake City, and we speak on a daily basis. Bill and Judith live in Cincinnati. We speak several times a week. I have never met four siblings who enjoy a closer relationship. We talk of their children and

*Me, Bill, Carole, and
Judith, June 2010.*

grandchildren. We talk about politics, sports, current events, and the declining health of our father, who was stricken with Alzheimer's and Parkinson's diseases ten years ago. We discuss the restored gospel and our Church callings. We recall our childhoods and the lessons taught to us by our parents, particularly those taught by our departed mother. Never a day goes by that we don't reflect on the joy we will feel when we are reunited with her in the next life. How we miss her, and how we love her. The joy of family is abundantly evident in my life.

I miss my mother and think of her every day. I often reflect on the lessons she taught me and the love she showed me. But those are not just private thoughts. To honor her, I wanted to share those lessons and that love with those around me. Her legacy is not some distant feeling. It is an eternal part of who I am and what I believe to be true about the meaning of life and the purpose of our journeys.

I am very much my mother's son. I hold dear those things that were most precious to her: family, faith, and service. I still strive to make her proud. I know that she is aware of who I am and what

I do. I know that the lessons she taught me, she now teaches to throngs of others who need to hear her strong witness of the plan of salvation and feel her abiding love. I still feel her love, power, and influence. That will never change.

It is true that I am not married, and yet that reality does not weigh down on me. I simply choose not to dwell on my bachelorhood. I revel in the fact that I am loved by many friends. When I am having a bad day, or when I feel alone, I know that Heavenly Father will bless me with evidence that He is watching over me by putting me in touch with one of my extraordinary friends or family members who consoles me, listens to me, or inspires me. I am so grateful for my friends. On many days, they truly are heaven-sent messengers who bring me joy.

I also draw much joy from my work as an assistant attorney general. Every day there are new issues to analyze and resolve for my clients. I am assigned many cases that are heart-wrenching and quite traumatic, and it is extremely gratifying to resolve the problems and struggles of individuals with disabilities and to know that I am lightening their respective burdens by utilizing the skills and talents with which I have been blessed.

I relish going to court and engaging in passionate advocacy for my clients. I feel I represent them tenaciously, and the joy that comes from obtaining justice for my clients is almost indescribable. To listen to a judge's verdict or decision on a particular case and to have that judge view the case the way that I view the case is exhilarating. It feels as though I just won the Super Bowl.

Recently, I was involved in a case involving three profoundly disabled brothers who had been living in deplorable conditions and who were now living in much better circumstances and receiving around-the-clock care. Their right to that care had been challenged, and after a two-day trial, the judge ordered that the men should

With Carole and Utah Governor Bangerter,
1993, on Steve Mikita Day.

remain where they could continue to live safely and actively. I wept with joy as I rolled out of the courtroom. It was one of those experiences that puts all of life into perspective. It was true joy!

I experience the simple joy of praying without kneeling. I still have access to a constant and consistent, loving Father in Heaven.

I love being able to eat. I can no longer chew, but I can still enjoy the taste of pureed food. I know that may not sound very appetizing, but to experience differing tastes in my mouth not only nourishes me but fills me with great happiness.

I cannot be left alone for extended periods of time during the day, as a result of the risk posed by my swallowing difficulties. Thus, I have very little privacy left. In fact, there are only one or two hours out of each day where I am able to enjoy total, uninterrupted privacy. I relish the tranquility of being alone. It gives me the opportunity to think, collect my thoughts, and sometimes even rest my very active brain. I am sure the day will come in the very near future when those two hours will decrease to mere minutes. But, as I have learned in living with my disease, even those minutes will provide

With Duke basketball coach
Mike Krzyzewski, 1993.

me with the joy that privacy brings. I am grateful for independent thoughts and the ability to be momentarily sequestered.

Although I cannot write and cannot turn the pages of a book or a newspaper, I find great joy in the ability to click a mouse in front of my computer at work or at home. What a blessing the computer age has brought to my life! I can satiate my love of current events and politics by reading news articles and editorials online. I am able to keep up on the daily wins and losses of my favorite sport teams, particularly the Duke Blue Devils and the Pittsburgh Steelers.

Most important, I can read the scriptures and conference talks online. I can enjoy them at my own pace and not worry about someone holding up my scriptures for me or sitting beside me and turning the pages of the *Ensign*. In fact, my knowledge of the gospel has increased as a result of the computer age. The Internet provides me with faster, greater access to the gospel library than anything that could be approximated in my home. Before the computer age, I was relegated to simply reading from books and magazines, and the strain that put on my body cannot be easily explained or overstated.

The computer is not just for entertainment. For me, it is both a lifeline and my primary vehicle to gaining and maintaining information, inspiration, and edification. It is truly a miracle, and I am constantly grateful for it.

Finally, there is one last focal point for the daily joy that I feel. It is simply the knowledge that I have acquired through the companionship of the Holy Ghost; He is the Revelator who testifies to me of the joyful truths that I hold so dear, and every time I write them, think of them, feel them, or utter them, I am filled with a feeling of peace and joy that cannot be experienced through any other manner, matter, or means found on this earth.

That feeling is both eternal and everlasting. It comes from a realm that is not confined to either time or space. It is that joy that cannot be limited by disease, weak muscles, or the dreaded departure of our loved ones. I know that He lives. He is the One whom Joseph saw in that grove of trees. He still stands as the King of Kings and Lord of Lords! He is still Wonderful, and He is my Counselor. He is my Advocate with the Father.

He never has forsaken me, forgotten me, or ignored me. He is the One who sweated great drops of blood in Gethsemane and did not shrink in the face of His suffering.

He still sees me as He sees you. He is the Great Jehovah of the Old Testament, and He is the Messiah of the New Testament, the Book of Mormon, and the Doctrine and Covenants. He is the light and the life and the joy of us all. He is Jesus the Christ, the Son of the Living God; that knowledge is irreplaceable, and the joy that He continues to bring to me, and to all of us, is unparalleled in its power and majesty. How grateful I am to have lived long enough to know Him, to testify of Him, and to love Him.

POSTSCRIPT

On June 24, 2010, my father passed away after languishing for the last three years from the ruthless combination of Alzheimer's and Parkinson's. Knowing that his mortal life was drawing to a close, I telephoned one of my closest friends, who lives in Hollywood, California, seeking her comfort and counsel; both her mother and grandmother died from Alzheimer's.

I explained to her that Dad was failing, but I did not know what to expect in these last hours. Her response startled me. She said, "Stevie, it has already happened. I have felt the power of your father's spirit all day."

When I ended our phone call, I immediately contacted Bill and Judy, who were at Dad's bedside in Ohio. Bill picked up the phone immediately and said, "We think Dad just took his final breath." He then said, "Fifty-two seconds . . . Sixty seconds . . . Seventy-five seconds . . . One minute thirty seconds. Steve, Dad's gone."

I telephoned my sister, Carole, so that she could join us on the phone.

There we all were—connected by phone inside the room of our powerful patriarch, William Brezuch Mikita—united as a family. We rejoiced, knowing that Dad was finally reunited with his eternal sweetheart and our dear mother.

SOURCES CITED

Ashton, Marvin J. "Progress through Change," *Ensign,* November 1979, 61–63.

Bednar, David A. "Ask in Faith." *Ensign,* May 2008, 94–97.

Eyring, Henry B. "Education for Real Life." *Ensign,* October 2002, 14–21.

"The Family: A Proclamation to the World." *Ensign,* November 1995.

Hymns of The Church of Jesus Christ of Latter-day Saints. Salt Lake City: The Church of Jesus Christ of Latter-day Saints, 1985.

Maxwell, Neal A. "Enduring Well." *Ensign,* April 1997, 7–10.

Monson, Thomas S. "'Behold Thy Mother.'" *Ensign,* January 1974, 29–32.

Smith, Joseph. *History of The Church of Jesus Christ of Latter-day Saints.* 7 vols. Edited by B. H. Roberts. Salt Lake City: The Church of Jesus Christ of Latter-day Saints, 1932–51.

———. *The Personal Writings of Joseph Smith.* Compiled and edited by Dean Jessee. Salt Lake City: Deseret Book, 1984.

Young, Brigham. Quoted by George H. Brimhall in "The Brigham Young University." *Improvement Era* 23, no. 9 (July 1920): 831–33.

ABOUT THE
AUTHOR

Steve Mikita graduated magna cum laude in Political Science and Religion from Duke University and received a juris doctorate from Brigham Young University's J. Reuben Clark Law School. He has served as an assistant attorney general for the State of Utah for more than twenty years and has appeared more than forty times before the Utah Supreme Court.